Rossiter Johnson

A History of the War of 1812-15

Between the United States and Great Britain

Rossiter Johnson

A History of the War of 1812-15
Between the United States and Great Britain

ISBN/EAN: 9783337013318

Printed in Europe, USA, Canada, Australia, Japan

Cover: Foto ©ninafisch / pixelio.de

More available books at **www.hansebooks.com**

CHAPTER II.

THE DETROIT CAMPAIGN.

First Bloodshed—Attitude of Political Parties—Plans for Invading
Canada—Capture of Michilimackinac—Engagements at the River
Raisin and Maguaga—Battle of Chicago—Hull's Surrender.

IT was perhaps characteristic of the conduct of
the war, that the first blood spilled should be
American blood, shed by Americans. This occurred
in a riot, occasioned by high party feeling, and it is
a curious fact that it took place in the same city
where the first blood was shed, also by riot, in the
great war of the Rebellion, half a century later. In
the night of June 22d, three days after the proclamation of war, a mob in Baltimore sacked the office
of the *Federal Republican*, edited by Alexander
Hanson, because he had opposed the war policy.
The mob also attacked the residences of several
prominent Federalists, and burned one of them.
Vessels in the harbor, too, were visited and plundered. About a month later Hanson resumed the
publication of his paper, and in the night of July
26th the mob gathered again. This had been expected, and Hanson was ready for them. A large

number of his friends, including Generals James M. Lingan and Henry Lee, offered to assist him in protecting his property. When the rioters burst into the building, they were at once fired upon, and one of them was killed and several were wounded. The authorities were slow and timid in dealing with the riot ; and when at length a force of militia was called out, instead of firing upon the mob, or capturing the ringleaders, they arrested Hanson and his friends, and lodged them in jail. The rioters, thus encouraged by those whose business it was to punish them, attacked the jail the next night, murdered General Lingan, injured General Lee so that he was a cripple for the rest of his life, and beat several of the other victims and subjected them to torture. The leaders of the mob were brought to trial, but were acquitted !

In this state of affairs, the war party in the country being but little stronger than the peace party, the youngest and almost the weakest of civilized nations went to war with one of the oldest and most powerful. The regular army of the United States numbered only six thousand men ; but Congress had passed an act authorizing its increase to twenty-five thousand, and in addition to this the President was empowered to call for fifty thousand volunteers, and to use the militia to the extent of one hundred thousand. Henry Dearborn, of Massachusetts, was made a major-general and appointed to command the land forces. Against the thousand vessels and one hundred and forty-four thousand sailors of the British navy, the Americans had twenty war-ships and a few gunboats, the whole carrying about three hundred guns.

But these figures, taken alone, are deceptive; since a very large part of the British force was engaged in the European wars, and the practical question was, what force the United States could bring against so much as England could spare for operations on the high seas and on this side of the Atlantic. In that comparison, the discrepancy was not so great, and the United States had an enormous element of strength in her fine merchant marine. Her commerce being temporarily suspended to a large degree, there was an abundance both of ships and sailors, from which to build up a navy and fit out a fleet of privateers. Indeed, privateering was the business that now offered the largest prizes to mariners and ship-owners. Yet so blind was President Madison's Administration to the country's main strength and advantage, that he actually proposed to lay up all the naval vessels, as the only means of saving them from capture. Of what use it would be to save from capture war-vessels which were not to sail the sea in time of war, he seems not to have thought. From this fatal error he was saved by the pluck and foresight of Captains Stewart and Bainbridge. Those two officers happened fortunately to be in Washington at the time, and succeeded in persuading the Administration to give up this plan and order the vessels fitted for sea at once.

War with Great Britain being determined upon, the plan of campaign that first and most strongly presented itself to the Administration was the conquest of the British provinces on our northern border. This had been attempted during the Revolution without success, but none the less confidence was felt in it now. And it was certainly correct in principle, though it proved wofully disastrous in the execution. It is observable that in all recent wars, the party on whose ground the fighting has taken place has been in the end the losing party. Thus the Mexican war in 1846-7 was fought in Mexican territory, and the Mexicans were defeated. The Crimean war was fought in Russian territory, and the Russians were defeated. The war between France and Austria, in 1859, was fought in Austrian territory, and the Austrians were defeated. The Schleswig-Holstein war was fought in Danish territory, and the Danes were defeated. The war between Prussia and Austria, in 1866, was fought in

Austrian territory, and the Austrians were defeated. The Franco-German war of 1870 was fought in French territory, and France was defeated. The Russo-Turkish war of 1877 was fought in Turkish territory, and the Turks were defeated. The war of the American Rebellion was fought in territory claimed by the rebels, and they were defeated. It only needs that a war should continue long enough for us to see where the battle-ground is to be, and we can then tell what will be its result. The reason is obvious. A nation that is strong enough to carry the war into its enemy's country, and keep it there, will certainly prove strong enough to win in the end, unless interference by some other power prevents it ; while a nation that is too weak to keep war, with all its devastation and ruin, out of its territory, must certainly be defeated unless assisted by some neighboring people. The invaders may, and probably will, lose the greater number of men in the pitched battles ; but it is not their harvests that will be trampled, not their mills that will be burned, not their bridges that will be blown up, not their homes that will be desolated, not their families that must fly for shelter to the caves and the forests. Their sources of supply are untouched. This principle was recognized by Scipio, when he declared that the war with Carthage "must be carried into Africa."

As England claimed to be mistress of the seas, and practically the claim was almost true, the determination to send our little navy and a fleet of privateers against her was essentially carrying the war into English territory. And as this part of the contest was conducted with skill and valor, it was gloriously successful.

An invasion of Canada being determined upon, the first question that necessarily arose was, at what point that country should first be attacked. To any one not skilled in military science the most obvious plan would seem the best—to march as large a force as possible, without delay, into Canada at the nearest point. A young officer, Major Jesup, of Kentucky, sent a memorial to the Secretary of War, in which he set forth a totally different plan from this. He proposed that a strong expedition should be fitted out to capture and hold Halifax, which was then a city of fifteen thousand inhabitants, with the most important harbor in the Canadian provinces. As a precedent, he could refer to the capture of Louisburg in 1748. But the Secretary, Hon. William Eustis, of Massachusetts, spoke of it contemptuously as "a very pretty plan," and set it aside. Yet it was sound in principle, and if properly carried out could hardly have failed to secure important results. In striking an enemy on the flank, it is always desirable to choose that flank by which he holds communication with his base. A blow on the other flank may inflict injury, but it only drives him back toward his base. A movement that cuts him off from such communication compels him either to surrender or to fight at great disadvantage. Canada's base — for many supplies, and largely for soldiers — was England. The port of Quebec was frozen up nearly half the year, and the occupation of Halifax by an American force would have gone far toward severing the connection between the provinces and the mother country. That harbor, too, was all-important for the refuge and refitting of British naval vessels on this side of the Atlantic.

Looking at the matter as purely a military problem, it was a pity that this brilliant plan was not adopted. But in a larger consideration it is probably fortunate for us that it was not. It might have resulted — indeed, that was contemplated in the plan — in leaving the Americans, at the close of the war, in possession of Canada. As the structure of our government almost precludes the holding of conquered provinces as such for any length of time, the Canadas must have soon become States of the Republic. But, so far from that being desirable in 1815, it may be doubted whether even yet the time has arrived when it would be wise to incorporate that undesirable population, in a body as they are, with the people of the United States.

In planning for the invasion of Canada, the Administration counted largely upon a supposed readiness of the Canadians to throw off their allegiance to Great Britain and join with the United States. Such expectations have almost never been realized, and in this instance they were completely disappointed.

In the preceding February, William Hull, Governor of the Territory of Michigan, who had rendered distinguished service in the Revolution, had been made a brigadier-general and placed in command of the forces in Ohio, with orders to march them to Detroit, to protect the Territory against the Indians, who were becoming troublesome. In June he was in command of about two thousand men, in northern Ohio, moving slowly through the wilderness. On the day when war was declared, June 18th, the Secretary of War wrote him two letters. The first, in which the declaration was not mentioned, was despatched by a special messenger, and reached General Hull on the 24th. The other informed him of the declaration of war, but was sent by mail to Cleveland, there to take its chance of reaching the General by whatever conveyance might be found. The consequence was, that he did not

receive it till the 2d of July. But every British commander in Canada learned the news several days
earlier.

Hull arrived at Detroit on the 5th of July, and set
about organizing his forces.   On the 9th he received
from the War Department orders to begin the invasion of Canada by taking possession of Malden, ·
fifteen miles below Detroit, on the other side of the
river, if he thought he could do so with safety to his
own posts.

He crossed on the 12th, and issued a proclamation to the Canadians.   In this he told them that
he came to do no injury to peaceable citizens, who
might remain at their homes and pursue their usual
occupations in security ; that he neither asked nor
needed their help, but would accept the services of
such as might volunteer ; and that no quarter would
be given to any who adopted Indian modes of warfare or were found fighting in company with the
savages who were accustomed to scalp prisoners and
murder non-combatants.   After the campaign had
resulted disastrously, General Hull was censured and
ridiculed for this proclamation ; but a copy had been
transmitted to the Secretary of War, and approved
by him ; and indeed, if a proclamation was to be
issued, it is difficult to find any serious fault with
Hull's.   The error was in issuing any at all — a

thing which a general seldom does with any good effect.

Hull fortified his camp on the east side of the river, and while waiting for his artillery sent out reconnoitring parties toward Fort Malden, and detachments to bring in supplies. As his troops grew impatient, he called a council of war, explained the situation to his officers, and offered to lead them in an attempt to carry the fort by storm, without waiting for artillery, if they thought their men could be relied upon for such an enterprise. Colonel Miller answered that his regiment of regulars could be depended upon for anything they might be ordered to do ; but the three militia colonels very wisely answered that raw militia could not be expected to storm a fortified place, unaided by artillery — one of the most hazardous of all military exploits.

So it was decided to defer the attack, and in a few days came the news that on the declaration of war, a force of over six hundred—British and Indians—had promptly moved against the American post at Michilimackinac—on the rocky little island of Mackinaw, commanding the strait between Lake Huron and Lake Michigan—and the garrison of sixty-one officers and men capitulated on the 16th of July. This disaster to the Americans roused the Indians to renewed hostility against them, while it proportionately disheartened Hull, and seems to have been the first step in the breaking down of his courage. After a few skirmishes, he recrossed to Detroit on the 7th of August.

Meanwhile the British Colonel Proctor had arrived, at Malden with reënforcements, and on Hull's withdrawal to Detroit he threw a force across the river to intercept his supplies. This force consisted of a small number of British regulars and a considerable number of Indians commanded by the famous Tecumseh. Learning that a supply train, accompanied by a few volunteers, was coming to him and had got as far as the River Raisin, about thirty-five miles south of Detroit, General Hull sent out a detachment of about two hundred men, under Major Thomas B. Van Horne, to meet it and escort it to camp. This detachment was attacked by the British and savages at Brownstown, twenty miles from Detroit. Van Horne was surprised, and retreated to the edge of a wood. His men behaved badly, and could not be got into line, another retreat was ordered, and finally they ran away in confusion, having lost eighteen killed, twelve wounded, and seventy missing.

Hull sent out another detachment, of six hundred men, under Lieutenant-Colonel James Miller, to open communication with the supply train, which was more fortunate. At **Maguaga**, fourteen miles from Detroit, they came upon the enemy intrenched behind a breastwork of logs. The British were commanded by Major Muir, the savages by Tecumseh. Miller at once ordered a bayonet charge, which his men executed in gallant style. The enemy were driven from their works, after some hard fighting, and pursued for two miles. They finally reached their boats, and crossed to Malden, but nearly a hundred Indians lay dead on the field, and the English had lost fifteen killed and forty wounded. The American loss was fifteen killed and sixty wounded. Instead of pushing on to the River Raisin, and securing the supplies, Colonel Miller returned with his command to Detroit.

As the direct road on which all these operations had taken place lay along the river-bank, in sight of the enemy and exposed to the fire of his gunboats, Hull now sent out a detachment under Colonels **McArthur** and **Cass**, to escort the train by a circuitous route, farther from the river.

During this gloomy state of things at Detroit, a bloody affair took place on ground that is now within the city of Chicago. Fort Dearborn stood at the mouth of Chicago River, and was occupied by a garrison of about fifty soldiers, with several families. Captain Nathan Heald, commanding the post, had been ordered by General Hull to abandon it and remove his force to Detroit. With so small a force, moving more than two hundred miles through a wilderness in time of war, it was especially desirable to retain the good will of the Indians. Captain Heald accordingly called a council of those who professed to be friendly, told them of his intended movement, and promised to give them all the property in the fort that he could not take with him, at which they were greatly pleased. But in the night, knowing their intemperance and fearing their treachery, he destroyed all the alcohol, firearms, and gunpowder which he could not take away. These were the very articles that the Indians most highly valued, and when, after his departure next morning (August 15th), they discovered the trick that had been played them, they were very much enraged, and hurried on to overtake him. He was moving slowly southward along the shore of the lake, when the crest of a low range of sand-hills on his right was suddenly lighted up with a blaze of musketry. The savages were there in ambush, mercilessly firing upon the little caravan. As quickly as possible the wagons were drawn up together, and the women and children given shelter in and behind them, while the soldiers stood their ground, and returned the fire of the Indians. It was a brave and bloody fight, and when some of the men had fallen the women took up their rifles and fired upon the savages with all the courage and coolness of soldiers. But after heavy losses, the survivors of the party were compelled to surrender. In the course of the fight, an Indian had made his way to the wagons, and, springing into one in which twelve children had been placed, tomahawked every one of them. The victorious savages scalped all the wounded, claiming that they had not been included in the capitulation, and the bloody trophies were sold to Colonel Proctor, who had offered a premium for American scalps.

The fight near Fort Dearborn took place on the same day that the detachment under Colonels McArthur and Cass left Detroit. The next day, August 15th, the British General Isaac Brock, who had arrived at Malden a few days before and assumed command there, formally demanded the surrender of Detroit. This demand included a plain threat of massacre in case of refusal. Said Brock in his letter : " It is far from my intention to join in a war of extermination ; but you must be aware that the numerous bodies of Indians who have attached themselves to my troops will be beyond my control the moment the contest commences." This is a fine example of the art of putting things. The reader would suppose from Brock's words—" the Indians who have attached themselves to my troops"—that the savages in red skins had insisted on accompanying the expedition in spite of the most strenuous efforts on the part of the savages in red coats to shake them off ; whereas Brock had just held a formal council with the Indians, and regularly arranged the terms of alliance. Two years later, when peace was being negotiated, the British commissioners spoke of these Indians, not as an irresponsible force, but as regular allies, who must share in the treaty.

General Hull gave a defiant reply, ordered McArthur and Cass to return at once with their detachment, and made admirable arrangements to defend the place. In the afternoon there was an artillery duel between two twenty-four pounders in the fort and a British battery at Sandwich on the opposite side of the river.

Brock's force, according to his own testimony, numbered 1330 men, including 600 Indians, and he had also two ships of war. Hull had present for duty about 1000 men.* Brock sent a large body of Indians across the river that night, at a point five

---

* It is impossible to reconcile the conflicting statements as to the numbers on either side.

miles below the fort, and early in the morning crossed with the remainder of his troops, and at once
marched on the place.   Hull had posted his regulars
in the fort, and his militia in the town, where the
stout palings that surrounded the little kitchen gar-
dens gave them an admirable shelter.   The two
twenty-four pounders were loaded heavily with grape
and placed so as to command the road by which the
enemy was approaching, in close order, twelve deep.
Never was there a better opportunity to do whole-
sale execution by a single discharge.   Everybody was
watching in breathless expectation to see the match
applied and the murderous iron go surging through
those beautiful ranks, when, to the astonishment of
friend and foe alike, a white flag was hung out upon
the wall of the fort.   Brock himself was surprised,
when, sending to know what it meant, he learned
that Hull had determined to surrender.   The articles of capitulation were drawn up, and the American general surrendered not merely the fort and its
garrison, but the whole Territory of Michigan, of
which he was Governor.   Thus ended this miserable
campaign.

Hull's officers were incensed at his action, and he
was subsequently court-martialled, convicted of
cowardice, and condemned to death ; but the
President pardoned him, in consideration of his

age and his services in the Revolution. The points
of his defence were : that an army in a situation
like his, cut off from its supplies, must surrender
sooner or later ; that if he had given battle, it
would have exposed all the inhabitants of the Territory to Indian barbarities ; that his situation was
the fault of the Administration, rather than his own ;
that his force was inferior to Brock's ; and that his
provisions were nearly exhausted. Benedict Arnold
himself was hardly held in greater contempt by the
American people than was General Hull for years
after his trial. Many believed him to be more
traitor than coward. This state of feeling was
largely due to Colonel Lewis Cass — nearly forty
years later a candidate for the Presidency — who
hurried to Washington with the news, and greatly
exaggerated the circumstances that bore against
Hull. Cass's action in this matter was exceedingly
discreditable. On one point, the important question of supplies, a letter written by him two days
before the surrender was flatly contradicted by his
testimony at the trial. Subsequent investigations,
if they do not exonerate General Hull, have at least
greatly modified the blame attached to him.

CHAPTER III.

FIGHTS WITH THE INDIANS.

Tecumseh's Scheme—Harrison's March to Fort Wayne—Defence of
Fort Harrison—Defence of Fort Madison—Ball's Fight.

THE great Indian leader, Tecumseh, cherished a design similar to that of Pontiac in the previous century. He wanted to unite all the northwestern tribes in an effort to drive the white man out of the country, or at least out of the Northwestern Territory. For the prosecution of this design the disasters which the Americans had sustained in the fall of Michilimackinac, Fort Dearborn, and Detroit seemed an auspicious opening, and Tecumseh endeavored to follow it up promptly with attacks on the other frontier posts held by United States troops. The most important of these were Fort Wayne, on the present site of Fort Wayne, Indiana, and Fort Harrison, on the Wabash, above Terre Haute.

A force of Kentuckians had been gathered in August and placed under command of General William Henry Harrison, afterward President of the United States, destined for the reënforcement of

Hull at Detroit.   But after the news of his surrender, it was directed to the relief of Fort Wayne, to
reach which required a long march through the wilderness of western Ohio.   A journal kept by one of
the soldiers on this march, Elias Darnell, is still
extant.   It contains many amusing and suggestive
anecdotes.   Under date of September 5th he says :

" General Harrison, having paraded the remaining part of the army in a circle in close order, delivered a speech to them, stating that he had just
received intelligence from Fort Wayne ; that it was
in great danger of being taken by the Indians and
British ; he said that we were under the necessity of
making a forced march to their relief.   He read
some of the articles of war, and stated the absolute
necessity of such regulations and restrictions in an
army, and if there were any who could not feel willing to submit to those articles and go on with him,
they might then return home.   One man, belonging
to Colonel Scott's regiment, made a choice of returning home, rather than submit to those terms.
Some of his acquaintances got a permit to escort him
part of the way home.   Two of them got him upon
a rail and carried him to the river ; a crowd followed
after ; they ducked him several times in the water,
and washed away all his patriotism."   The danger
from firearms in the hands of undisciplined volun-

teers is shown by these passages : " One of Captain McGowen's company was accidentally shot through the body by one of the sentinels." " A man was accidentally shot through the head by one of the mounted riflemen." " One of the light horsemen wounded a man as he was feeding his horse, believing him to be an Indian." The privations of such an expedition are well illustrated by this : " We marched through some first-rate woodland, and through a prairie of the best quality. It is badly watered ; the water in the wagon-ruts was the only drink we could get to cool our scorching thirst, and but very little of that." And the romantic incidents by this : " The tomb of a chief was discovered ; it was built on the ground with timber and clay, so that no rain or air could enter. The chief was laid on his blanket, his head toward sunrise, his rifle by his side, his tin pan on his breast, with a spoon in it ; he was ornamented in their style, with ear-rings, brooches, etc."

Fort Wayne, which was well provisioned and had a garrison of about seventy men, commanded by Captain Rhea, was besieged by the Indians for two weeks. A portion of General Harmar's expedition had been defeated by the savages on this spot twenty-two years before. The fort now had four small field-pieces, and was otherwise well equipped.

The Indians at first professed to be friendly, and tried by all means to surprise the garrison. Then they mounted logs to look like siege guns. But the wary Captain Rhea was not to be deceived, and on the approach of Harrison's expedition, September 12th, the besiegers decamped. Their villages and cornfields in the neighborhood were destroyed.

Fort Harrison was less fortunate than Fort Wayne. It was commanded by Captain Zachary Taylor, who was afterward President of the United States. His force was very small, and had been reduced by sickness to about fifteen effective men. On the 3d of September two young settlers were killed and scalped near the fort by Indians. The next day thirty or forty of the savages appeared with a white flag, asked for admission to the fort, and wanted something to eat. Taylor had been warned to expect an attack, was on his guard, and refused to open the gates. Near midnight a block-house which formed part of the outer line of fortifications was found to be on fire. The crowd of savages outside was now swelled to several hundreds, and what with their horrible yelling and the cries of nine women and children inside the fort, and the rapidly spreading flames, the little garrison was thrown into considerable confusion. The destruction of the block-house would open a gap through which the

Indians would quickly pour in a swarm, and then woe
to the little band of whites ! But Captain Taylor
never lost his coolness for a moment. He ordered
the part of the roof of the barracks which was nearest to the fire to be thrown down, and the end of
the barracks kept wet. The invalids and convales-
cents manned the two bastions and the other block-
house, and kept up a fire on the Indians, to protect
the men who were at work on the roof. This fight
against a double foe was kept up for eight hours ;
and the garrison not only prevented the fire from
spreading, but erected a temporary breastwork to
cover the gap made by the destruction of the block-
house, and thus completely foiled the Indians, who
disappeared next day, driving off as many as possible
of the cattle belonging to the neighboring farmers.
Of the garrison, two men were killed and two
wounded. For this skilful and gallant action, Taylor was made a major. A passage in his official report of the affair is interesting, not as having any
bearing on the result, but because by detailing the
experience of two individuals it gives us a vivid idea
of the manner in which such contests were conducted. He says : " One man lost his life by being too
anxious ; he got into one of the galleys in the bastions, and fired over the pickets, and called out to
his comrades that he had killed an Indian, and,

neglecting to stoop down, in an instant he was shot dead. One of the men that jumped the pickets returned an hour before day, and, running up toward the gate, begged for God's sake for it to be opened. I suspected it to be a stratagem of the Indians to get in, as I did not recollect the voice ; I directed the men in the bastion, where I happened to be, to shoot him, let him be who he would ; and one of them fired at him, but fortunately he ran up to the other bastion, where they knew his voice, and Dr. Clark directed him to lie down close to the pickets, behind an empty barrel that happened to be there, and at daylight I had him let in. His arm was broke in a most shocking manner, which he says was done by the Indians—which I suppose was the cause of his returning. The other they caught about one hundred and thirty yards from the garrison, and cut him all to pieces.''

Fort Madison, which had been built in an exposed and badly chosen situation on the bank of the Mississippi, near the site of St. Louis, was attacked on the 5th of September by more than two hundred Indians, Winnebagos. They approached stealthily, caught one of the garrison outside of the fort, and shot and scalped him within sight of his comrades on the walls. Firing was kept up on both sides for two days, but with little effect. On the 7th the savages displayed on poles the head and heart of the man they had killed, and later in the day tried to destroy the buildings by shooting upon the roofs arrows to which they had tied combustible matter and set it on fire.   As at Fort Harrison, the appearance of fire created a panic among the men ; but the commander, Lieutenant Hamilton, was equal to the occasion.   He ordered eight old gun-barrels to be made into syringes, and small holes to be broken through the roof from the inside.   Thrusting up the syringes through these holes, the men were able in a few minutes to make the roof as wet as if a heavy shower had fallen, which completely baffled the design of the enemy.   On the 8th the Indians took possession of an old stable near the fort, and renewed the fight ; but a few cannon-shot were sent crashing through the stable, while the gun-barrel syringes did duty as before, and the savages then withdrew.

Besides these actions at the forts, there were numerous encounters between small parties of white men and Indians, in which often great skill and courage were displayed.   One of the most noteworthy was Colonel Ball's fight.   That officer was descending the bank of Sandusky River with twenty-two mounted men, when a party of Indians about equal to their own numbers fired upon them from ambush. Ball and his men charged into the ambuscade, drove out the savages, and killed the chiefs. Ball was dismounted, and struggling with a gigantic chief, when one of his men came up and shot the Indian. The remaining Indians then became furious, and gave the signal for no quarter. Ball's men understood the situation, and fought without flinching, till they had killed every one of their antagonists. This affair had a wholesome effect upon the Indians of that region, and for some time the settlers were unmolested.

CHAPTER IV.

THE BATTLE OF QUEENSTOWN.

Fight at Gananoqui—Expedition against Ogdensburg—Elliott captures two War-vessels—Gathering of Forces on the Niagara—Battle of Queenstown—Death of General Brock.

HULL'S surrender by no means put an end to the design of invading Canada, but neither did it have any effect in changing the vicious plan of striking the enemy on the wrong flank.

In the night of September 20th, Captain Benjamin Forsyth embarked at Cape Vincent, New York, with about a hundred men, and in the morning landed near the village of Gananoqui, Canada. Here an engagement took place with about an equal number of British troops—regulars and militia—at the close of which the enemy fled, leaving ten men dead on the field and several wounded and prisoners. Captain Forsyth then burned the military storehouse—which was the object of his expedition—paroled the captured militia, and returned to the American shore with a few regulars as prisoners of war and a considerable quantity of arms and ammunition. One man of his party had been killed.

In retaliation, the Canadians fitted out a much more formidable expedition against **Ogdensburg.** It consisted of about seven hundred and fifty men, who on the 2d of October embarked in forty boats, and under the escort of two gunboats moved up the St. Lawrence. At the same time, the British batteries at **Prescott,** opposite Ogdensburg, opened fire on that place, which was returned by an American battery. The next day was spent in preparations, and in the forenoon of Sunday, the 4th, the final embarkation was made from Prescott, in twenty-five boats and the two gunboats. As a blind, they proceeded up the river past Ogdensburg for some distance. Then suddenly they turned about and bore down upon that place, while at the same instant the British batteries reopened fire on the village. The American battery, together with a company of riflemen, all under command of General Jacob Brown, reserved fire till the flotilla was within point-blank range, and then opened all at once. The fire was returned, and kept up steadily for an hour. Two of the boats were so damaged that they had to be abandoned, and another, with its crew, was captured. The expedition then returned to Prescott without having effected a landing on American soil.

In the surrender of Detroit was included the brig-of-war *Adams,* which left the Americans with no naval force whatever on the upper lakes. Lieutenant Jesse D. Elliott, of the navy, was sent to Buffalo to organize a flotilla, and soon after a detachment of sailors to man it was ordered thither from New York. In October the *Adams*, which the British had renamed *Detroit*, and a smaller vessel, the *Caledonia*, which had taken part in the capture of Michilimackinac, came down Lake Erie, and cast anchor near Fort Erie. Elliott formed a plan for their capture, and with a force of fifty sailors and fifty soldiers embarked in boats at midnight of the 8th. They rowed silently across the river, and before they were discovered leaped upon the decks of the vessels, secured the crews, weighed anchor, and headed for the American shore. As the wind was too light to carry them up stream, they were obliged to run down past the British batteries. The *Caledonia*, which had a valuable cargo of furs, was run ashore at Black Rock and secured. The *Detroit* fought the enemy's batteries while unsuccessful efforts were made to tow her beyond their reach. Finally she drifted ashore at Squaw Island, where her captors abandoned her, taking away their prisoners. A party of British soldiers subsequently boarded her, but were driven off by fire from a battery. In the course of the day she underwent a heavy fire from both sides, and in the evening a British party were preparing to recover her, when they were anticipated by an American party who boarded her and set her on fire.   For this exploit, in which half a dozen of his men were killed, Congress gave Lieutenant Elliott a vote of thanks and a sword.

These comparatively trifling incidents of border war were succeeded by one much more serious, though not more effective.   In the summer General Dearborn had entered into an armistice with Sir George Prevost, the British commander in Canada, which set free the enemy's troops on the Niagara frontier, who were promptly moved against Hull at Detroit.   That campaign being finished, a large part of them was drawn back to the line of the Niagara, and when in the autumn a movement in that quarter was contemplated by the Americans, they were confronted by a considerable force at every point where a crossing was possible, while General Brock, the victor of Detroit, was on the ground, commanding the whole, and ready to concentrate them at any point that might be attacked.   He expected the crossing to take place at the mouth of the river.

General Stephen Van Rensselaer, commanding all the forces on the American side of the Niagara, determined to cross from Lewiston, at the foot of the rapids, seven miles below the great Falls, and seize Queenstown.   The importance of the place arose from the fact that it was the terminus of the portage between Lake Ontario and the upper lakes. At this point the high ground through which the great chasm of the river below the Falls has been cut slopes down to a lower plateau, on which stands the village of Queenstown.

The British had one piece of artillery on the Heights, south of the village, and another on the bank of the river a mile below. It was believed by many that General Van Rensselaer, who had been a prominent Federalist, was opposed to the war and purposely delayed moving against the enemy. Whether this was true or not, the discontent with his tardiness was so loudly expressed and had begun so to demoralize his troops, that at last he acknowledged himself compelled by it to move. He had minute information as to the situation and strength of each post of the enemy on the western bank of the river, and could choose his own point for crossing. He had about six thousand troops under his command—regulars, volunteers, and militia. The immediate command of the attacking force was assigned to his cousin, Lieutenant-Colonel **Solomon Van Rensselaer**, which occasioned serious dissatisfaction, because he was only an officer of New York militia, while some of the officers who had been ordered to join the expedition were commissioned in the United States regular army, and therefore ranked him.

Thirteen large boats, capable of carrying 340 men, with their equipments, were brought on wagons and launched at Lewiston on the 10th of October, and arrangements were made for crossing before daylight the next morning.

That night a cold, northeast storm set in, and the troops, who were promptly brought to the rendezvous, stood shivering for hours in the rain and darkness, on the river-bank, waiting for the boats, which did not come. At length day dawned, and the crossing had to be postponed. It afterward appeared that the boats had been intrusted to one Lieutenant Sims, who was said to have taken them up the river, far beyond the point at which they were wanted, and then abandoned the expedition. No sufficient motive has ever been assigned for this extraordinary conduct on the part of the lieutenant. It has been suggested that he was so incensed at seeing the command given to an officer of militia, that he was willing to destroy his own reputation, if he had any, for the sake of frustrating the movement.

Two days later the attempt was renewed. Three hundred regulars under Lieutenant-Colonel John Chrystie, and an equal number of militia under

Colonel Van Rensselaer, were to cross the river before daybreak of the 13th, and storm the Heights of Queenstown, and the remainder of the troops to follow and reënforce them. Lieutenant-Colonel **Winfield Scott** arrived from Buffalo on the evening of the 12th, and asked leave to join the expedition, but was refused. Yet he placed a battery on Lewiston Heights, to protect the troops while they were crossing.

It was still cold and stormy when the embarkation took place. All the regulars and a few of the militia crossed, and ten of the boats returned for a second load. The other three boats, in one of which was **Chrystie**, had missed their way in going over.

A force of the enemy, under Captain **Dennis**, moved down promptly to resist the landing, and some of the Americans were killed or wounded before they stepped on shore. Captain John E. Wool, being the senior officer present, assumed the command, and quickly moved his troops up the bank, where they formed in line at the foot of the Heights. The enemy was reënforced almost at the same time, and attacked the Americans in front and on the right flank with artillery and musketry. Wool stood his ground, though he had no artillery, and a short but bloody fight ensued. Of the ten officers of regulars, two were killed, and four, including Wool himself, severely wounded.   The left wing was composed of the militia.   There the fighting was less severe, but Lieutenant-Colonel Van Rensselaer was so seriously wounded that he was obliged to withdraw from the contest and recross the river.   The steady and well-directed fire of Wool's men drove the enemy's left wing back into the village ; but his right wing, stationed on the Heights, was unmoved.   Annoyed by the fire from that quarter, the Americans fell back to the river-bank to re-form, and were soon re-enforced by another company of regulars.

Receiving leave, rather than orders, from Van Rensselaer to capture the Heights, Wool placed the fresh troops on his right, and set out upon the task, while Lieutenant Lush followed in rear of the column, with orders to shoot down any man who faltered.   Wool first moved his command southward along the water's edge, the bank sheltering them from the sight of the enemy, and then at the point where the gorge of the river made a sharp edge, as it were, to the Heights began the ascent, still out of sight of the battery-men.   In many places the pathway was so steep and rugged that the soldiers had to use their muskets like alpenstocks, and climb by seizing the bushes, and "boost" one another. Wool was foremost in the scramble, and near the top found a fisherman's path which led to the plateau,

and had been left unguarded because it was supposed to be impassable. By this path they gained
the summit, and silently filed out upon the plain to
the rear and right of the British battery.

Meanwhile General Brock, hearing the sounds of
battle, had ridden up rapidly from Fort George at
the mouth of the river, and now stood near this
battery, watching the operations below. A sudden
volley of musketry in the rear startled him, and the
appearance of Wool's column rushing down upon
the battery caused him to retreat down the slope
without waiting to mount his horse, followed by his
staff and the artillerymen, and their entire infantry
support. When the sun rose, a few minutes later, it
shone upon the American flag floating over the captured works.

Brock sent orders to General Sheaffe at Fort
George to bring up reënforcements, and at the same
time to open an artillery fire on Fort Niagara, on
the opposite bank; for the British commander had
been all the while of opinion that the movement on
Queenstown was but a feint, and that the real attack
would be made at the mouth of the river. Without
waiting for the reënforcements, Brock placed himself
at the head of the troops that had just been driven
from the Heights, and the troops in the village, and
attempted to recapture the lost position. As the

assaulting force moved up the slope, it bore to the west, to envelop the left flank of the Americans. Wool sent a detachment to check this movement; but his men were too few, and his whole command was forced back till it stood with a powerful enemy in front and a precipice behind it. At this point of time, a captain raised a white handkerchief on the point of a bayonet; but in an instant Wool tore it down with his own hands, and then, addressing a few inspiriting words to his men, he persuaded them to re-form their somewhat broken ranks, and keep up a steady and effective fire. When their ammunition was nearly exhausted, they made a gallant bayonet charge which drove the enemy down the slope.

Brock rallied his troops for another assault, received a few reënforcements, and was just setting the column in motion when a bullet struck his breast and he fell mortally wounded. His troops, now under command of **Lieutenant-Colonel McDonell,** rushed forward with the cry of "Revenge the General!" but to no purpose. Wool's little band stood firm, and drove back the enemy once more with serious loss, McDonell being mortally wounded, and the two officers next in command disabled, while ten men and an Indian chief remained with the Americans as prisoners. The troops who had accomplished this gallant feat were recruits who had never seen service before, and their leader, now but twenty-three years of age, had not received a military education, but was a bookseller and then a law-student, until commissioned as a captain.

About ten o'clock reënforcements were sent over to Wool, and Lieutenant-Colonels **Winfield Scott** and John Chrystie, and General William Wadsworth, soon followed them. The last-named officer, who was in plain clothes, modestly made known his rank, but insisted that the command should be assumed by Scott, whom he heartily and efficiently supported.* Wool was now, from loss of blood, obliged to withdraw from the field. Scott had about six hundred men — three hundred and fifty regulars and two hundred and fifty militia. He placed them in position to repel any attack of the enemy, and at the same time to cover the crossing of the remaining militia, which was to be sent over to him at once.

All this time General **Roger H. Sheaffe** was hurrying up from Fort George with troops, in obedience to the orders sent to him by Brock in the morning. He arrived on the field, and was ready for action

---

* He was uncle of General James S. Wadsworth, who was killed in the battle of the Wilderness in 1864.

about two o'clock. His entire force coinded,
about thirteen hundred soldiers and five hun.
Indians.

The militia on the American shore could overlook
the field of battle, and saw the approach of Sheaffe.
But when General Van Rensselaer attempted to
move them across the river to the support of their
victorious but hard-pressed countrymen, they refused to stir. The law provides that militia shall
not be compelled to serve beyond the bounds of the
State against their will ; the men fell back upon this
privilege, and all entreaty was in vain. This action
—or non-action—on the part of the militia has subjected them to severe censure, and has uniformly
been attributed to pure cowardice. But while it was
probably not altogether justifiable, there were some
circumstances, not generally mentioned, which partially excuse it. For instance, they knew that,
through gross mismanagement, all the boats, except
one small scow, had been allowed to float off down
the current or be captured by the enemy ; and hence
if they crossed it must be by a small boatload at a
time, instead of in a body.

In spite of this disappointment, Scott resolved to
make the best fight he could with what troops he
had. The first attack was made on his left flank by
the Indians, who were commanded by John██████t;

accomplished the Joseph Brant of Revolutionary fame.
Every attack Scott repelled with gallant bayonet
charges ; but when about four o'clock Sheaffe moved
up his whole force, and doubled back the right
flank, the Americans were obliged to retreat. A
few let themselves down the precipice, clambering
from ledge to ledge and from bush to bush, but
when they reached the water's edge there were no
boats to receive them. The greater part retreated
a short distance along the road leading from Queenstown to the Falls ; but seeing escape was impossible, they surrendered in a body. To do this, they
had to send a flag of truce through the line of Indians, and it was three times fired upon before it
finally reached the British commander. The last
time it was borne by Scott in person.

So ended the battle of Queenstown, which was a
very remarkable action, and with better management
might have had a different termination. General
Van Rensselaer, in his official despatches, labored
to create the impression that the refusal of the
militia to cross the stream was the whole cause of
the final disaster, and at the same time he studiously
avoided mentioning the names of the officers—Wool
and Scott—to whom was due the credit for all the
successes and glory of the day.

The Americans, in this series of engagements,

lost about ninety men killed, a hundred wounded, and nearly a thousand taken prisoners. The British loss has never been determined. The American prisoners were sent to Quebec, where twenty-three Irishmen were separated from the others and sent to England to be tried for treason, on the ground that they were British subjects and had been fighting against their own flag. As soon as the American authorities had an equal number of prisoners in their possession they placed them in close confinement, and gave notice that their fate would be determined by that of the twenty-three Irishmen. People who know nothing of historical experience in such matters always cry out against any proposal of retaliation, arguing that it will simply result in the murder of all the prisoners on both sides. As a matter of fact. when retaliation is promptly and firmly threatened for violation of the laws of war, it always has the effect of stopping the outrage. And so it proved in this case ; for twenty-one of the captured Irishmen lived to return to their adopted country. The other two died in prison.

During the funeral of General Brock, minute guns were fired by the Americans on the eastern bank of the river, "as a mark of respect to a brave enemy." There was perhaps no harm in this little bit of sentiment, though if the Americans remembered that two months before, in demanding the surrender of Detroit, General Brock had threatened to let loose a horde of savages upon the garrison and town, if he were compelled to capture it by force, they must have seen that their minute guns were supremely illogical, not to say silly.   Brownell, in one of his best poems, expresses the true sentiment for such a case :

> " The Muse would weep for the brave,
>   But how shall she chant the wrong ?
> When, for the wrongs that were,
>   Hath she lilted a single stave ?
> Know, proud hearts, that, with her,
>   'Tis not enough to be brave."

CHAPTER V.

WAR ON THE OCEAN.

The *President* and the *Little Belt*—The *President* and the *Belvidera*—
Hull's Race—The *Constitution* and the *Guerriere*—Effect of the
Victory—The *Wasp* and the *Frolic*—The *United States* and the
Macedonian—The *Constitution* and the *Java*—Nelson's Prediction.

WHILE the year 1812 brought nothing but disaster to the land forces of the United States, on the ocean it was fruitful of victories that astonished the world. It is greatly to the credit of President Madison that he followed the advice of Captains Stewart and Bainbridge, in opposition to his entire Cabinet, to develop and use the navy, instead of laying it up. That was not only the wise but the appropriate thing to do. This was pre-eminently a sailors' war, entered upon chiefly for the purpose of protecting American seamen from impressment in a foreign service, and its ultimate result would be a settlement of the question whether American ships were to be at liberty to sail the high seas at all, or whether, as a poet of our day puts it, the Atlantic Ocean was to be considered merely John Bull's back yard. It was the wise thing to do, because, if a nation determines to go to war at all, it should do it in earnest ; and the most effective war is made when the earliest and most persistent blows are directed at the enemy's vital part. Of all Great Britain's possessions that could be reached by balls or bayonets, her ships at sea were the most important to her. Canada might be overrun, or even conquered, and she would hardly feel its loss—or at least she could exist without it ; but anything that weakened her navy and deranged her commerce would make every Englishman feel the penalties of war.

A slight foretaste of what American seamanship and gunnery might do had been afforded by an affair that took place a year before the war broke out. The American frigate *President*, of forty-four guns, with Commodore John Rodgers on board, was cruising off Sandy Hook in May, 1811, searching for an English frigate that had taken a sailor from an American brig, when she sighted a strange craft. In answer to her hail, the stranger fired a shotted gun, and the shot struck the mainmast. The *President* promptly returned the fire, and in a few minutes broadsides and musketry blazed out from both vessels. As soon as Rodgers perceived the inferiority of his antagonist, he ordered his gunners to cease firing ; but no sooner were his guns silent than the stranger opened again. With another broads two the *President* completely crippled her, and then hailed and got an answer. As darkness now came on, Rodgers lay to for the night, keeping lights displayed, in case the stranger should need assistance. In the morning he sent an officer on board, who learned that she was the British ship *Little Belt;* that she was badly damaged, and had lost thirty-one men killed or wounded. But she declined receiving any assistance. On board the *President* one boy had been slightly wounded. Each vessel sailed for home, and each commander told his own story, the two accounts being widely different. The version here given is that of the American officers. According to the English captain, the *President* began the action by firing a broadside into the unoffending *Little Belt.* Each government accepted the statement of its own officers, and there the matter rested.

It was this same vessel, the *President*, that fought the first action of the war. With news of the declaration came orders to Commodore Rodgers, then in New York, to sail on a cruise against the enemy. Within one hour he was ready. The *Hornet*, of eighteen guns, Captain Lawrence, was ready at the same time, and the *Essex*, of thirty-two guns, Captain Porter, a few hours later.

About this time information had been received that a large fleet of British merchantmen had left Jamaica, under a strong convoy, for England, and on the 21st of June, Rodgers left the port of New York with his squadron, in search of them. He did not find them ; but on the morning of the 23d a sail appeared in sight, which proved to be the British frigate *Belvidera,* and the *President* gave chase. About four o'clock in the afternoon the vessels were within gunshot, and Rodgers opened fire with his bow-guns, sighting and discharging the first one himself. The ball struck the rudder-coat of the *Belvidera,* and passed into the gun-room. The next shot struck the muzzle of one of her stern-chasers. The third killed two men and wounded five. At the fourth shot the gun burst, blowing up the forecastle deck, on which Rodgers was standing, and hurling him into the air. The explosion also killed or wounded sixteen men. This caused a lull in the action, and the *Belvidera's* men went back to their guns and returned the fire with considerable effect. The *President* soon began to forge ahead, when the *Belvidera* cut loose her anchors, stove her boats and threw them overboard, started fourteen tons of water, and thus lightened, managed to escape, and a few days afterward made the port of Halifax. The total loss of the *President,* killed and wounded, in this action, was twenty-two ; that of the *Belvidera,* about half as many.

An English privateer was captured by the *Hornet* on the 9th of July, and subsequently seven merchantmen, and an American vessel that had been captured by the enemy was retaken.

When the *Belvidera* carried into Halifax the news of the declaration of war, and that the American cruisers were out, a squadron of five vessels, under Captain Vere Broke in the *Shannon,* was sent out to destroy Rodgers. They did not find him, but they captured several American merchantmen off the port of New York, and also took, after a smart chase, the little brig-of-war *Nautilus.*

The *Essex,* which had left port a little later than the *President* and *Hornet*, took several prizes, one of them being a transport filled with soldiers. She was chased by the *Alert,* of twenty guns, and fired upon. The *Essex* was armed with carronades, guns not intended for work at long distances. Waiting till the enemy had come pretty near, she suddenly opened her broadside, and in eight minutes the *Alert* struck her colors.

The great war-game on the ocean began in earnest when Captain Isaac Hull sailed from the Chesapeake in July, in the *Constitution*, a frigate of forty-four guns. On the 17th he came in sight of five vessels, which proved to be Broke's squadron, and the next day he was surrounded by them. As the wind was very light, he resorted to " kedging" to keep out of reach of them. This consisted in sending a boat ahead for perhaps half a mile, with a kedge anchor and lines. The kedge was then dropped, and the lines carried back to the ship. These being fastened to the windlass, the crew, by turning it and winding them up, pulled the vessel up to the anchor. While this was being done, the boat was going ahead with another kedge and lines, to repeat the operation and make it continuous. The flagship of the British squadron was pretty close in chase when the American frigate was thus seen to be walking away from it. The enemy soon found out how the mysterious movement was made, and resorted to the same expedient. But it was not possible to approach very near by this means, as it would have brought his boat under the fire of the American's stern-guns. Captain Hull had cut away some of the woodwork and run two twenty-four pounders out at his cabin windows, and also mounted a long gun on his spar deck as a stern-chaser. Whenever there was a little wind, every vessel set every stitch of canvas she could carry, and all the nicest arts of seamanship were resorted to to gain the slightest advantage. Eleven ships were in sight most of the time, all participating in the contest. An American merchantman appeared to windward, and the British vessels, not wishing to leave the chase, displayed an American ensign to decoy her within reach of their guns. Thereupon the *Constitution* hoisted an English flag, to warn her off. This exciting race was kept up for three days. In the evening of the second day, it was evident that a heavy squall was coming up. Just before it struck the *Constitution*, all the light canvas was furled, and the ship was brought under short sail in a few minutes. When the pursuing vessels observed this, they began at once to let go and haul down without waiting for the wind. Presently the squall came, and with it a rainstorm that hid the vessels from one another. As soon as this happened, the *Constitution* sheeted home and hoisted her fore and main topgallant sails, and while her pursuers were steering in different directions to avoid the force of the squall, and believed her to be borne down by the pressure of the wind, she was sailing straight away from them at the rate of eleven knots an hour. When the squall was over, the nearest vessel of the British squadron was seen to be a long way astern, and to have fallen off two points to leeward, while the slowest ones were so far behind as to be almost out of sight. The chase was kept up during the night, but in the morning was found to be so hopeless that it was abandoned.

This contest, though a mere race, attended with

no fighting, no damage of any kind, and only a
negative result, is famous in the annals of the ocean.
It was a fine instance of that superior seamanship
which stood the American sailor in good stead
throughout the war, and contributed quite as much
as his valor to the brilliant victories that rendered
Great Britain no longer the mistress of the seas.

Hull made sail for Boston, and after a short stay
in that port sailed again on the 2d of August. He
cruised along eastward as far as the Gulf of St.
Lawrence, where he captured and . burned two
small prizes, and then stood southward. In the
afternoon of the 19th a sail was descried from the
masthead, and the *Constitution* at once gave chase.
Within an hour and a half she was near enough to
the stranger to see that she was a frigate ; and a little later she laid her maintopsail aback and waited
for the *Constitution*, evidently anxious for a contest.

Hull immediately put his vessel in complete trim
for a fight, cleared for action, and beat to quarters.
At five o'clock the English frigate, which proved to
be the *Guerriere*, of thirty-eight guns, Captain
Dacres, hoisted three ensigns and opened fire. The
Constitution approached cautiously, so as to avoid
being raked, firing occasionally, but reserving most
of her guns for close action.

After an hour of this, the *Guerriere* indicated her

readiness for a square fight, yard-arm to yard-arm, and the *Constitution* set her sails to draw alongside. The fire from both ships became gradually heavier, and in ten minutes the mizzen-mast of the *Guerriere* was shot away. The *Constitution* then passed slowly ahead, keeping up a constant fire, her guns being double shotted with grape and round shot, and attempted to get a position across the bows of the enemy and rake her. But in trying to avoid being herself raked while gaining this position, she luffed short, and fell foul of her enemy. At this moment the cabin of the *Constitution* took fire from the flash of the *Guerriere's* guns, and for a while it looked as if she would fare hardly. But by the energy and skill of **Lieutenant B. V. Hoffman**, who commanded in the cabin, the fire was extinguished, confusion prevented, and a gun of the *Guerriere* that might have repeated the mischief disabled.

The instant the vessels came together, each attempted to board the other ; but a close and deadly fire of musketry prevented. On the American side, Lieutenant Morris, Master Alwyn, and Mr. Bush, Lieutenant of Marines, sprang to the taffrail to lead their men, when they were all shot down. Finding it impossible to board, the *Constitution* filled her sails and shot ahead, and a moment later the *Guerriere's* foremast fell and carried the mainmast with it. This reduced her to a wreck, and as a heavy sea was on she was helpless. The *Constitution* hauled off a short distance, repaired damages, and at seven o'clock wore round and took a position for raking. An ensign that had been hoisted on the stump of the mizzen-mast was at once hauled down in token of surrender, and the prize was won. A lieutenant sent on board returned with the news that she was one of the squadron that had so lately chased the *Constitution*.

The victor kept near her prize through the night, and at daylight the officer in charge reported that the *Guerriere* had four feet of water in the hold and was in danger of sinking. Captain Hull therefore transferred the prisoners to his own vessel, recalled the prize crew, and set the wreck on fire. In fifteen minutes the flames reached the magazine, and the hulk that still remained of the proud English frigate was blown to pieces.

In this battle the *Constitution* lost seven men killed and seven wounded. Her rigging suffered considerably, but her hull was only very slightly damaged. The *Guerriere* lost seventy-nine men killed or wounded. The location of this battle may be found by drawing a line directly east from the point of Cape Cod, and another directly south from Cape Race; the point of intersection will be very near the battle-ground. It is a little south of the track of steamers between New York and Liverpool.

The news of this victory was a startling revelation, on both sides of the Atlantic. In expressing their contempt for the American navy, the English journals had especially ridiculed the *Constitution*, as "a bunch of pine boards, under a bit of striped bunting." This bunch of boards had now outsailed a squadron of eleven British war-vessels, and in a fight of half an hour had reduced one of their frigates to a wreck and made her strike her colors. It was true that the American ship was slightly superior in number of men and guns ; but this would not account for the superiority of seamanship, the better gun-practice, and the enormous difference in losses. Captain Dacres, who was afterward put on trial for losing his ship, asserted that he had sent away a considerable number of his men in prizes ; that he had several Americans in his crew who refused to fight against their countrymen, and that he permitted them to go below. But all allowances that could be made did not change the essential character of the victory. Only a short time before, the London *Courier* had said, "There is not a frigate in the American navy able to cope with the *Guerriere*."

Captain Hull, who was now in his thirty-eighth year, had entered the navy at the age of twenty-

three, and had gained distinction in the war with
Tripoli.   When he landed in Boston with his prisoners, nearly the whole population of the town
turned out to greet him.   Flags and streamers were
displayed on every hand, decorated arches spanned
the streets, and a banquet was spread for him and
his crew.   He made a sort of triumphal progress to
New York and Philadelphia, where similar honors
were paid him, and handsome swords and snuff-
boxes presented to him.   Congress voted him a gold
medal, to each of his commissioned officers a silver
medal, and fifty thousand dollars to the crew as
prize money.

In his official report the Captain said : " It gives
me great pleasure to say that, from the smallest boy
in the ship to the oldest seaman, not a look of fear
was seen.   They all went into action giving three
cheers, and requesting to be laid close alongside the
enemy."   The London *Times* said : " It is not
merely that an English frigate has been taken, after
what we are free to confess may be called a brave resistance, but that it has been taken by a new enemy,
an enemy unaccustomed to such triumphs, and
likely to be rendered insolent and confident by
them.   He must be a weak politician who does not
see how important the first triumph is, in giving a
tone and character to the war.   Never before in the

history of the world did an English frigate strike to an American ; and though we cannot say that Captain Dacres, under all circumstances, is punishable for this act, yet we do say there are commanders in the English navy who would a thousand times have rather gone down with their colors flying than have set their brother officers so fatal an example.''

The next naval contest, in the order of time, was that of the *Wasp* and the *Frolic*, one of the bloodiest of the war. The *Wasp*, an American sloop-of-war, of eighteen guns, commanded by Captain **Jacob Jones**, was a very fast sailer, and had gone to Europe with despatches, when the war broke out. On her return she was refitted with all haste and sent out on a cruise. In the night of October 17th, about five hundred miles off **Cape Hatteras**, she sighted a fleet of six English merchantmen under convoy of the *Frolic*, a brig, of twenty-two guns, **Captain Whinyates**. Four of the merchantmen were armed.

The next morning, the sea being somewhat rough, the *Wasp* was put under short canvas and got into fighting trim, and then bore down upon the *Frolic*, which kept herself between her convoy and the enemy. She also was under short canvas, and her main-yard was on deck. About half past eleven o'clock the *Wasp* came up close on the starboard side of the *Frolic*, and broadsides were exchanged at the distance of only sixty yards. The fire of the Englishman was the more rapid, but that of the American was the more deliberate and effective. In a little over four minutes the *Wasp's* maintopmast was shot off and with the maintopsail-yard fell across the braces, rendering the head-yards unmanageable. A few minutes later her gaff and mizzen-topgallant-mast were shot down ; and before the action was over, every brace and most of the rigging was carried away. The shot of the *Wasp* was directed mainly at her enemy's hull, and the firing on both sides was kept up with great spirit, little or no attempt being made to manœuvre, and the vessels gradually approaching each other.   At last they were so near that the American gunners touched the side of the *Frolic* with their rammers, her bowsprit passed over the *Wasp's* quarterdeck, and the latter was brought directly across the Englishman's bows, in position for raking. Captain Jones ordered a broadside ; and when it was fired, the muzzles of two of the guns were actually in the bow ports of the *Frolic*, and the discharge swept her from stem to stern.

As no sign of submission had come from the enemy, Captain Jones was about to repeat the raking, but was prevented by the impetuosity of his crew. A sailor named John Lang, who had once been impressed on a British man-of-war, hot for revenge, sprang upon the bowsprit of the *Frolic*, cutlass in hand, and was followed by Lieutenant Biddle and an impromptu boarding-party. They met no opposition. Two or three officers, wounded and bleeding, were standing on the after-part of the deck ; there was a cool-headed old seaman at the wheel ; and dead and wounded sailors were lying about in all directions. The officers threw down their swords, and Lieutenant Biddle sprang into the rigging and hauled down the British flag. The battle had lasted forty-three minutes. On board the *Wasp*, five men had been killed and five wounded. The loss on the *Frolic* has never been ascertained, it was at least seventy-five. Captain Whinyates, in his official report, said that not twenty of his men escaped injury.

The two vessels were separated, and in a few minutes both masts of the *Frolic* fell. Arrangements were made for sending her into Charleston with a prize crew, while the *Wasp* should repair damages and continue her cruise. But before this plan could even be fairly entered upon, the British ship-of-the-line *Poictiers*, carrying seventy-four guns, hove in sight, and speedily made prize of both vessels and took them to Bermuda.

On the same day when this action took place,

Commodore Stephen Decatur, cruising in the frigate *United States*, captured the British packet *Swallow*, which had on board a large quantity of specie.   He continued his cruise eastward, and only a week later (October 25th), at a point about midway between the Azores and the Cape Verd Islands, sighted a large vessel to windward, which proved to be the English frigate *Macedonian*, carrying forty-nine guns, Captain Carden.   She was somewhat smaller than the *United States*, and had fewer men.   Decatur made up to the stranger ; but she had the advantage of the wind, and for some time managed to keep out of reach.   At length, after considerable manœuvring, the distance was shortened, and both vessels opened fire with their long guns.   The gunnery of the American was superior, and while sustaining little injury herself she inflicted serious damage upon her antagonist.   At the end of half an hour, the distance had been still more diminished, so that the carronades were brought into use.   A carronade is a short gun, throwing a comparatively large ball with not very great velocity.   The size of the ball and its slower motion cause it to splinter and tear a ragged hole in the side of a ship, where a smaller shot with a greater velocity would pass through and make a smooth round hole, which could easily be plugged up again.

As the *Macedonian* became disabled, she fell off to leeward, while the *United States* passed ahead and to windward, and then tacked and came up under her lee. The firing, which had been entirely with artillery, now ceased on both sides. The *Macedonian's* mizzen-mast was gone, her main and foretopmasts carried away, her main-yard cut in two, and her ensign had disappeared. The *United States* hailed her, and was answered that she had struck her colors. She had received a hundred shot in her hull, most of them in the waist. She went into the action with three hundred men, of whom she lost thirty-six killed and sixty-eight wounded. On board were seven impressed American sailors, two of whom were killed. On the *United States* five men were killed and seven wounded. Her rigging was considerably cut, but otherwise she received very little injury.

Decatur took his prize to New York, going in by way of Long Island Sound, where he arrived on New Year's day, 1813. He was received with a great ovation, and there were banquets, orations, and public rejoicings unlimited. Congress, following the precedent set in the case of Hull, voted a gold medal to the commander, and a silver one to each of his commissioned officers.

A member of the British Parliament, making a

speech concerning this affair, said he '' lamented that, with the navy of Great Britain against that of America, which consisted of only four frigates and two sloops, two of our finest frigates were now in their possession, captured by only two of theirs. This was a reverse which English officers and English sailors had not before been used to, and from such a contemptible navy as that of America had always been held, no one could suppose such an event could have taken place.''

And the London *Independent Whig* was constrained to say : '' A powerful and rival nation is now rapidly rising in the west, whose remonstrances we have hitherto derided, but whose resentment we shall soon be taught to feel ; who for our follies or our crimes seems destined to retaliate on us the miseries we have inflicted on defenceless and oppressed states, to share with us the fertile products of the ocean, and snatch from our feeble and decrepit hands the imperial trident of the main.''

But the cup of English humiliation was not yet full. The Americans had another able commander, with a stanch ship and a fearless crew, who now came in for his turn. This was Commodore William Bainbridge, who sailed from Boston late in October, on board the *Constitution*, the same vessel with which Hull had conquered the *Guerriere*. In company with her sailed the brig *Hornet*, of eighteen guns, commanded by Captain James Lawrence.

They cruised southward, and in December the *Hornet* was left at San Salvador, or Bahia, Brazil, to blockade an English brig that was on the point of sailing with a large amount of specie on board. Lawrence had sent in a challenge to fight the two brigs, on even terms, just outside the harbor, but the English captain declined.

The *Constitution* continued her cruise, and on the 29th, off the Brazilian coast, sighted the English frigate *Java*, carrying thirty-eight guns, Captain Lambert. Bainbridge tacked and drew the stranger off the land, which was not more than thirty miles distant, and when far enough away stood toward him. The enemy seemed quite as anxious for a contest, and about two o'clock it began. The firing was heavy and continuous. The *Java* had the advantage of the wind, and attempted to cross the *Constitution's* bow, to rake her. But the latter wore, and avoided it. This manœuvre was repeated several times, and at length the *Constitution*, though her wheel had been shot away, making it difficult to manage the steering-gear, succeeded in getting the coveted position, and raked her antagonist.

The *Java*, which had been badly damaged, ran down upon the *Constitution* with the intention of boarding. But her jibboom became entangled in the *Constitution's* mizzen-rigging, and she was held there and raked mercilessly. At this time her bowsprit and foremast were shot away.

The two vessels now separated, and after considerable manœuvring came together again, yard-arm and yard-arm, and reopened their broadsides. Now the *Java's* mizzen-mast tumbled, and her main-mast was the only stick left standing. The *Constitution* then hauled off, and spent an hour in repairing damages, at the end of which time she wore round and stood across her antagonist's bow, when the English colors were struck.

The action had lasted an hour and fifty-five minutes. The *Constitution* had lost nine men killed and twenty-five wounded, Commodore Bainbridge being slightly wounded. The loss on board the *Java* was variously stated ; the lowest estimate made it twenty-two killed and one hundred and one wounded. Bainbridge said that sixty were killed. Captain Lambert was mortally wounded. The whole number on board was four hundred, including General Hislop and his staff and other officers, who were on their way to the East Indies.

The *Java* was a complete wreck, and after a day or two it was determined to blow her up, which was done after all the prisoners and wounded had been carefully removed. She might have been towed into Bahia ; but Brazil was friendly to Great Britain, and Bainbridge did not want to trust his prize in a Brazilian harbor. He, however, landed his prisoners there, and paroled them.

The *Constitution* — which received the name of "Old Ironsides," on account of escaping serious damage in this action — arrived at Boston in February. Here the same welcome that had been given to Hull and Decatur was extended to Bainbridge. The cities of New York and Albany gave him gold snuff-boxes, Philadelphia gave him a service of silver, and Congress voted the usual medals, with fifty thousand dollars of prize money for the crew.

In the first six months of the war, the little American navy, for which Congress had done nothing, and from which nothing had been expected, had six encounters with English cruisers, and in every one was victorious. These defeats were a sore trouble to English naval historians, who have ever since been laboring to explain them away. They have invented all sorts of ingenious theories to account for them ; but it has never occurred to them to adopt the simple explanation that they *were* defeats, brought about by superior seamanship and gunnery, backed up by the consciousness of a just cause, on the part of the Americans. The favorite explanation has been, that the American so-called frigates were seventy-four-gun ships in disguise ; that the English crews were all green hands, and their numbers were not full at that. A few years later, General Scott met at a dinner in London a young British naval officer, who superciliously inquired, "whether the Americans continued to build line-of-battle ships, and to call them frigates." "We have borrowed a great many excellent things from the mother country," answered Scott, "and some that discredit both parties. Among the latter is the practice in question. Thus when you took from France the *Guerriere*, she mounted forty-nine guns, and you instantly rated her on your list a thirty-six-gun frigate ; but when we captured her from you, we found on board the same number, forty-nine guns !"

During this same half year, nearly three hundred British merchantmen had been captured and brought into American ports. In this work the little navy had been assisted by a large number of privateers, which had sailed from our ports, under letters of marque, and had not only helped themselves to the rich spoils of British commerce, but had occasionally fought with armed cruisers.

These disasters were no more than had been predicted by Lord Nelson, the greatest of English admirals. After watching the evolutions of an Ameri-

can squadron commanded by Commodore Richard
Dale, in the bay of Gibraltar, he is reported to have
said to an American gentleman who was on board
his flagship that " there was in those transatlantic
ships a nucleus of trouble for the maritime power of
Great Britain.   We have nothing to fear from anything on this side of the Atlantic ; but the manner
in which those ships are handled makes me think
that there may be a time when we shall have trouble
from the other.''

CHAPTER VI.

MINOR BATTLES IN THE WEST.

Winchester's Expedition—Fight at Frenchtown—Massacre at the
Raisin—Siege of Fort Meigs.

AT the opening of the year 1813, General William
Henry Harrison, who had won a high reputation by
his victory over the Indians at Tippecanoe in 1811,
being now in command of the forces in the West,
endeavored to concentrate them for a movement
against the British and savages at Detroit and Malden. An expedition composed mainly of Kentucky
troops, under General James Winchester, was making its way northward through Ohio to join him ;
and Leslie Coombs, of Kentucky, accompanied by
a single guide, went through the woods more than a
hundred miles on foot to inform Harrison of their
approach.

When Winchester's expedition reached the rapids
of the Miami, he was met by messengers from the
pioneers about the River Raisin, informing him that
the enemy was organizing a movement against the
settlements there, and imploring him to protect
them. A detachment of six hundred and sixty men,

under Colonels Lewis and Allen, was sent forward, and pushing on with the greatest possible rapidity, marching a part of the way over the frozen surface of Lake Erie, reached Frenchtown, on the Raisin, where Monroe, Michigan, now stands, on the 18th of January.

That place had been occupied a few days before by a hundred English and four hundred Indians, who now took the alarm and prepared to resist the advancing expedition. As he approached the village, Colonel Lewis formed his command in columns, and moved forward in the face of a heavy fire of musketry and artillery. The enemy was posted behind the houses and garden fences of the village, which stood on the north side of the river ; and the Americans, who had no artillery, crossed over on the ice and at once made a charge. Finding themselves attacked vigorously in front and on the left flank at the same time, the British retreated about half a mile, and took a new position in the woods, where they were partly protected by fallen timber. Colonel Lewis sent a detachment to strike this position on its right flank ; and as soon as he heard the firing there, Colonel Allen attacked it in front. The enemy retreated slowly, fighting at every step, and the Americans steadily pressed their advantage till dark, when they returned to the village and encamped. They had lost twelve men killed and fifty-five wounded. The loss of the enemy was not ascertained, but they left fifteen men dead on the field where the first engagement took place.

The news of this victory was sent at once to General Winchester, who came up promptly with a reënforcement of two hundred and fifty men. It was expected that the place would be attacked by a heavier British force from Malden, which was but eighteen miles distant, and preparations were made for constructing a fortified camp. But the enemy came before this could be completed. In the night of January 21st, Colonel Henry Proctor, with a force of about eleven hundred, British and savages, moved from Malden, and early in the morning of the 22d the American sentries were surprised. No pickets had been thrown out, and the troops were hardly brought into line when a heavy fire of artillery and small arms was opened, both in front and on the flanks, the yells of the savages being heard in the intervals of the discharges.

The attack in front was met and repelled by a steady fire, the Americans being considerably sheltered by the stout garden fences. On the right flank the attack was not so well resisted, and that wing was soon broken. It was rallied by Winchester, and reënforced by Lewis; but the enemy, seeing his advantage, followed it up, and the whole wing, reën-forcements and all, was swept away, the remnant retreating in disorder across the river.

All efforts to rally the fugitives were vain, and in a little while the Indians overwhelmed the left wing also. The disorganized troops of this wing attempted to escape by a road that led to the rapids of the Raisin ; but the savages were posted all along behind the fences, and shot down great numbers of them. They then took to the woods directly west of the village ; but here also were savages lying in wait, and it is said that nearly a hundred were tomahawked and scalped before they had gone as many yards. One party of nearly twenty men surrendered, but all except the lieutenant in command were at once massacred by their treacherous captors. Another party of forty were overtaken after they had retreated three miles, and compelled to surrender, when more than half of them were murdered in cold blood. General Winchester and Colonel Lewis were captured by the Indians, but Proctor, with some difficulty, got them under his protection. Colonel Allen, after trying without success to rally his men, retreated alone nearly two miles, and there sat down on a log, being too much enfeebled by wounds to go farther. An Indian chief came up and demanded his surrender, promising protection ; but almost immediately followed two others, who evidently intended to scalp him. Allen killed one of them with a single blow of his sword, and was immediately shot by the other.

Meanwhile the centre of the American line could not be dislodged from its position behind the fences. It was composed of Kentucky sharpshooters, and some idea of the havoc they made among the British regulars may be gained from the fact that out of sixteen men in charge of one gun thirteen were killed. Appalled at such losses, Proctor bethought him of a cheaper method than continued fighting. He represented to General Winchester, now a prisoner in his hands, that unless an immediate surrender were made, the result would be a complete massacre of the Americans. Winchester's fears were so wrought upon that he sent, by a flag of truce, orders to Major Madison to surrender. As he had no right to give orders of any kind while a prisoner in the hands of the enemy, Madison refused to obey, but offered to surrender on condition that safety and protection should be guaranteed to him and his men. When Proctor found he could not get the place in any other way without a great sacrifice of his troops, he agreed to the terms proposed, and the surrender took place.

But no sooner had the gallant little band become

prisoners, than Proctor, like many other British officers of that day, forgot his promise, and the savages began to plunder the prisoners, unhindered by their English allies. Thereupon the Americans resumed their arms, and by a vigorous bayonet charge drove off the Indians.

The next day the British force started for Malden, taking with it all the prisoners who were able to march. The badly wounded were left at Frenchtown, with no guard but a British major and the interpreters. The injured men were taken into the houses, and attended by two American surgeons. On the morning of the 23d, about two hundred Indians who had accompanied Proctor as far as Stony Creek, and there had a carouse, returned to Frenchtown, held a council, and resolved to kill all the prisoners who could not march away with them. They then proceeded at once to plunder the whole village, tomahawk the wounded men, and set fire to the houses. They perpetrated such outrages and cruelties that most of the historians have shrunk from detailing them. Many prisoners who managed to crawl out of the burning buildings were thrown back into the flames. A few of the strongest were marched off with the savages toward Malden ; but as one by one they became exhausted, they were mercilessly tomahawked and scalped. These scalps were carried to the British headquarters, where the savages received the premium for them.

Of the American force engaged in this affair, three hundred and ninety-seven were killed, five hundred and thirty-seven were prisoners, and but thirty-three escaped. The British are said to have lost twenty-four killed and a hundred and fifty-eight wounded. The loss of the Indians is unknown.

After the disaster at the River Raisin, General Harrison concentrated his remaining troops—twelve hundred men—and built Fort Meigs, at the foot of the rapids of the Maumee. This work was on the right bank of the stream, on high ground, and en-closed about eight acres. There were several strong block-houses, and considerable artillery.

General Proctor, with a force of about one thousand British and twelve hundred Indians, and two gunboats, set out on an expedition against this post in April. He crossed the lake, ascended the river, and on the 28th landed about two miles below the fort, but on the opposite bank. Here he erected a battery, and subsequently he planted two others, above the fort but on the left bank, and one below and very near it on the right bank. The Indians, commanded by the famous Tecumseh, were landed on the right bank, to invest the fort in the rear. The batteries opened fire on the 1st of May, and kept it up steadily four days ; but it had very little effect, owing largely to a traverse twelve feet high and twenty feet thick which the garrison had constructed while the batteries were being erected. Proctor on the third day demanded a surrender, with the usual threat of massacre.

Learning that General Green Clay was coming to him with a reënforcement of eleven hundred Kentuckians, Harrison had sent word to him to hurry forward as fast as possible. At midnight on the 4th of May, two officers and fifteen men from this force descended the river and entered the fort, with the news that Clay was but eighteen miles distant. Harrison sent orders to him to send eight hundred of his men across the river at a point a mile and a half above the fort, thence to march down the left bank and capture and destroy the enemy's batteries ; the remaining three hundred to march down the right bank and fight their way through the Indians to the fort.

The detachment landed on the left bank, commanded by Colonel Dudley, moved silently down upon the British batteries, and then, raising a terrific yell, were upon them before the enemy could realize that he was attacked. The guns were spiked and their carriages destroyed ; but instead of crossing to the fort at once, as Harrison's orders directed, the victors, flushed with their success, were drawn into a running fight with some Indians, and finally fell into an ambush, and all but about a hundred and fifty were either captured or killed. That number reached their boats and crossed.

The detachment on the right bank, under General Clay himself, had some difficulty in landing, and lost a few men in fighting its way through the Indians, but ultimately reached the fort. While these movements were going on, three hundred and fifty men of the garrison, under Colonel John Miller, made a sortie against the battery on the right bank, captured it, spiked the guns, and returned with forty-three prisoners.

When Clay's troops reached the fort, they were joined by another sallying party, and the combined force moved against the Indians, whom Tecumseh commanded in person, and drove them through the woods at the point of the bayonet. Tecumseh attempted to move a force of British and Indians upon their left flank and rear, to cut off their return to the fort, but this movement was frustrated by Harrison, who understood Indian warfare quite as well as the great chief himself.

Proctor's savage allies, disgusted at his want of success, now began to desert him, and he was obliged to raise the siege and retreat. This he did not do, however, without keeping up his reputation for treachery and cold-blooded cruelty. His prisoners were taken to old Fort Miami, a short distance down stream, where the savages were allowed to murder more than twenty of them. Captain Wood, an eye-witness, says : " The Indians were permitted to garnish the surrounding rampart, and to amuse themselves by loading and firing at the crowd, or at any particular individual. Those who preferred to inflict a still more cruel and savage death selected their victims, led them to the gateway, and there, under the eye of General Proctor, and in the presence of the whole British army, tomahawked and scalped them." It is said that the horrible work was stopped by Tecumseh, who, coming up when it was at its height, buried his hatchet in the head of a chief engaged in the massacre, crying : "For shame ! — it is a disgrace to kill a defenceless prisoner !" " In this single act," says the witness who narrates it, " Tecumseh displayed more humanity, magnanimity, and civilization than Proctor, with all his British associates in command, displayed through the whole war on the northwestern frontiers."

The total loss to the Americans in these actions was eighty-one men killed, two hundred and sixty-nine wounded, and four hundred and sixty-seven made prisoners. It is uncertain what the British loss was, but it was probably somewhat smaller than that of the Americans.

In July, Proctor and Tecumseh, with a combined English and savage force of about five thousand, returned to Fort Meigs and attempted to draw out the garrison by strategy ; but Harrison was, as usual, too shrewd for them, and they turned their attention to Fort Stephenson.   This was an oblong stockade fort, about a hundred yards long and fifty yards wide, with high pickets, surrounded by a deep ditch or moat.   There was a strong block-house at each corner.   It was on the Sandusky, where the town of Fremont, Ohio, now stands.   The garrison consisted of one hundred and sixty men, commanded by Major George Croghan.

The British sailed around into Sandusky Bay, and up the river, while their savage allies marched over-land and invested the fort in the rear, to prevent the approach of reënforcements.   Harrison believed the fort to be untenable, and had sent orders to Croghan to abandon and destroy it ; but these orders did not reach the Major till retreat had become impossible.

On the 1st of August Proctor sent in a flag of truce, and demanded an immediate surrender, accompanied with the usual threat that if it were refused the Indians would massacre the entire garrison as soon as the place was taken. The ensign who met the flag made answer that Major Croghan and his men had determined "to defend the fort, or be buried in it." Proctor opened fire from his gunboats and four guns which he had placed in battery on shore, and bombarded the fort continuously for two days and nights. As this fire was directed mainly against the northwest angle, Croghan expected the main attack to be made at that point, and prepared for it. Besides strengthening the walls with bags of sand and bags of flour, he placed his only gun, a six-pounder, where it would enfilade the ditch on that side, loaded it with a double charge of slugs, and masked it.

It was after sunset on the 3d when the storming parties approached. Two columns passed around the western side of the fort, to threaten the southern face, while a third, commanded by a Lieutenant-Colonel Short, approached the northwest angle. When it was within twenty yards, the Kentucky riflemen gave it a volley that thinned the ranks, but did not stop its progress. The Lieutenant-Colonel and a large number of his men scaled the outer line of pickets, and poured into the ditch. "Now, then," he shouted, "scale the pickets, and show the d——d Yankee rascals no quarter !"

The next moment, Croghan's single piece of artillery was unmasked and fired. It completely swept the ditch, cutting down nearly every soldier in it, while a volley of rifle-balls finished the bloody work. Lieutenant-Colonel Short, who was mortally wounded, immediately raised his handkerchief on the point of his sword, to ask for quarter.

Another column of red-coats attempted the task at which the first had so wofully failed, and the deadly performance of the howitzer and the rifles was repeated. The columns that approached the fort on the south were driven off by a single volley, and the battle was ended. In the night the British gathered up their dead and wounded, and the next morning they were seen to sail away, leaving behind a quantity of military stores. They acknowledged a loss of twenty-seven killed and seventy wounded ; but it was probably much larger. One American was killed, and seven wounded.

CHAPTER VII.

WAR ON THE LAKES.

The Armaments—Preliminary Operations—Expedition against York —Death of General Pike—Capture of Fort George—Attack on Sackett's Harbor—Battle of Stony Creek.

THE importance of the great navigable lakes lying between the United States and Canada had not been overlooked by either party to this war. As soon as it broke out, both began preparations to secure the ascendency on those waters—which, besides its direct advantages, would be almost necessary to either in making invasions around the coasts. A large portion of the shores on both sides—more especially, perhaps, on the American side—was at that time a wilderness, and the few open ports would naturally hold out strong temptations to the enemy.

The chief advantage was with the British, both because the oldest and largest settlements were on their side of the lakes, and because they had possession of the St. Lawrence River, which made it easy for them to bring up supplies from the seaboard. The Americans, however, had regularly trained naval officers in command of their few vessels on

lakes Ontario and Champlain, while the English had
not.   The largest American vessel on the lower lakes
was the *Oneida*, of sixteen guns ; the largest British vessel, the *Royal George*, of twenty-two.   The
enemy also had several other vessels, carrying from
a dozen to sixteen guns each, which it would be useless to specify, as their names and character were
several times changed during the war.   As soon as
hostilities were declared, both sides began building
new ships and arming merchant schooners.

In July, 1812, the British fleet had made an
attempt to capture the *Oneida* and a prize schooner,
both of which were at Sackett's Harbor.   Lieuten-
ant-Commander Woolsey anchored the *Oneida* in
the harbor, where she could command the entrance,
placed half of her guns in a battery on shore, and
easily drove off the enemy's fleet, whose performance exhibited very little of the character of serious
warfare.

In October, of that year, Captain Isaac Chauncey
arrived at Sackett's Harbor, with authority to organize a fleet.   He brought from New York forty ship-
carpenters and a hundred officers and seamen, and a
supply of naval stores.   He bought ten or a dozen
schooners, armed them—generally with long swivel
guns—and fitted them up for naval service as well as
their character would admit.   These, with the

Oneida, carried forty guns and four hundred and thirty men.

Chauncey's first exploit with this fleet was to chase the *Royal George* into the harbor of Kingston, and attack the batteries there ; but nothing was accomplished by it save the capture of two small prizes. He lost one man killed and eight wounded — five by the bursting of a gun. About the same time (November, 1812), an expedition was made to clear the Canadian shore of batteries at the head of Niagara River. Four hundred soldiers and sailors, commanded by Lieutenant-Colonel Bœrstler and Captain King, crossed from Black Rock in twenty boats, assaulted the batteries, and after desperate fighting captured them. They then spiked all the guns, burned the barracks, and retreated to the shore. The usual bad management seems to have entered into this, as into all the other enterprises of the sort, and the boats were not at hand for the re-crossing ; in consequence of which Captain King and sixty of his men were made prisoners.

Nothing can be done on the lakes in winter, as the harbors are closed by ice ; but the building of vessels went on, and with the opening of spring General Dearborn and Commodore Chauncey began operations which showed no lack of activity and energy, however well or ill judged they may have been.

York (now Toronto) was at this time the capital of Upper Canada. It was a place of about twelve hundred inhabitants, situated on a beautiful land-locked bay, about two by three miles in extent. The British were known to have a large vessel there, the *Prince Regent*, and to be building another. Mainly for the purpose of seizing this vessel, and destroying the one on the stocks, General Dearborn planned an expedition against York. He had seventeen hundred men available for the purpose, and Commodore Chauncey had fourteen vessels.

The expedition was organized, and sailed from Sackett's Harbor on the 25th of April. The winds were unfavorable, and the passage was somewhat tedious ; but the fleet arrived off the harbor of York on the 27th. The intention was to land the troops by means of boats, at a point about two and a half miles west of the town, the guns of the fleet covering the landing, and march at once on the defences of the place, where General Roger H. Sheaffe was in command. But the water was rough, and the boats were driven half a mile farther westward, where they were compelled to land with but little protection from the vessels.

Here a body of British and Indians, concealed in the edge of a wood, were ready to receive them.

A column of riflemen, under Major Forsyth, were

in the first boats, and as they approached the shore
the enemy opened upon them with a destructive
fire.   Forsyth lost a considerable number of men
before he could land.   But his riflemen stood up in
the boats and returned the fire with some effect,
and he was followed quickly by a battalion of infantry under Major King, and this by the main body
under General Zebulon M. Pike, who was in immediate command of the entire military force.   The
fleet at the same time contrived to throw a few
effective shots into the woods, and the landing was
effected without confusion.

The skirmishing party of British and Indians had
been gradually strengthened till, by the time General Pike's forces were on shore, they had an almost
equal force to dispute their passage toward the
town.   The enemy were still in the woods, and as
soon as the Americans had been formed in battle
order they advanced.   The nature of the ground
made it almost impossible to move or use their artillery ; but the enemy had three pieces, with which
they attacked the flanks of the column.   The fighting soon became hot and deadly.   There were
charges and counter-charges, one and another part
of either line alternately giving way and rallying
again ; but on the whole the advantage was with the
Americans, and the British were gradually forced

back into the outer defences.   The Indians are said to have fled from the field early in the action.

The approach to the town, along the shore, was crossed by numerous streams and ravines, and the enemy destroyed the bridges behind them as they retired.   Two pieces of artillery were with great difficulty taken across one of these ravines and placed where they could be brought to bear on the enemy.

The orders to the infantry were, to advance with unloaded muskets and carry the first battery at the point of the bayonet.   This was easily done, as the enemy only remained long enough to discharge two or three cannon-shots hastily, and then fell back to his second battery, nearer the town.

General Pike led the column forward at once to the second battery, which the enemy also abandoned, after spiking the guns.   Here he discovered that the barracks, three hundred yards still nearer to the town, appeared to be evacuated.   Suspecting that there might be some scheme on the part of the enemy for drawing him into a disadvantageous position, where a stand would be made, he halted at the second battery, and sent forward Lieutenant Riddle with a few men to find out the true state of affairs.

The Lieutenant found the barracks deserted, and was about to return with the information, when suddenly the ground was shaken by a terrific explosion, and in a moment the air was darkened by flying boards, timbers, and stones, bars of iron, shells, and shot. The magazine, containing five hundred barrels of powder, had been blown up. It was situated in a little ravine, the bank of which protected Lieutenant Riddle's party, all of whom escaped. But a considerable number of the beams and masses of masonry, passing over their heads, fell within the battery. General Pike, who had just been removing a wounded prisoner to a place of safety, at the moment was seated on a stump, questioning a British sergeant who had been captured in the woods. As the shower of débris came down within the battery, the General was crushed to the earth by a section of stone wall, and two of his aides and the wounded sergeant were also struck down — all of them being fatally injured. By this explosion, fifty-two Americans were killed outright, and one hundred and eighty wounded. About forty British soldiers also, who were near the magazine, were killed.

General Pike being disabled, the command devolved upon Colonel Cromwell Pearce, who pushed on with his troops as soon as possible, though not in time to prevent the escape of the British General Sheaffe and all his regulars who remained unharmed. Sheaffe drew up terms of capitulation, and left

them in the hands of the officer who commanded
the militia. As the Americans approached the
town, they were met by this officer with the offer to
surrender, the capitulation to include the town and
all government stores therein. While the parley
was going on, Sheaffe destroyed most of the military
stores, set fire to the war-vessel that was on the
stocks, and made off, but his baggage and private
papers were captured. Two hundred and ninety
officers and men—of the British navy and militia—
became prisoners and were paroled. General Pike
had enjoined upon his soldiers the duty of protecting private property in the town, and given orders
that marauding should be punished with death.
His wishes were carefully observed ; but the government buildings were burned.

General Pike, when his wound was found to be
mortal, was borne off to the fleet. A little while
afterward the British flag that had floated over York
was brought to him. He asked to have it placed
under his head, and in a few minutes calmly expired.
He was but thirty-four years of age, but had performed valuable services for his country, especially
in the command of two exploring expeditions, one
about the headwaters of the Mississippi, and the
other in what is now western Louisiana and Texas
—of both of which he published accounts.

The war-vessel that the Americans expected to capture at York had left the harbor two days before their arrival. The troops abandoned the place, and on the 1st of May were taken again on board the fleet, which as soon as the weather would permit, on the 8th, sailed away. In this expedition the loss of the American land forces was fourteen killed and twenty-three wounded, besides those who suffered from the explosion of the magazine. In the fleet, seventeen men were killed or wounded. The British regulars lost sixty-two killed and ninety wounded ; the loss of the Indians and militia was unknown.

Two episodes of this battle have been discussed with considerable warmth. The first is the explosion of the magazine. It is not certain that this was done purposely. General Sheaffe, in his report, attributed it to '' an unfortunate accident,'' but two English historians speak of it with commendation as a regularly laid plan. American writers who condemn it have done so on the ground that, as the commanding General had made arrangements for a surrender, the place was virtually surrendered already, and he therefore had no farther right to destroy life or even property. Commodore Chauncey probably gave the correct view of the matter when he wrote : '' I am much inclined to believe that General Sheaffe was correct when he stated that it was accidental.

Nor could I condemn the enemy, even if a train had been laid. It is a perfectly legitimate mode of defence, as every student of history knows ; and why should we censure the garrison for thus employing an acknowledged means of defence, to check the progress of an invader?" If the surrender had not virtually taken place, it is difficult to see why the defenders of the town are to be any more blamed for firing a stone wall at their enemy than they would have been for firing a thousand bullets.

The other point discussed is the burning of the government buildings. They were undoubtedly set on fire, though without orders from headquarters. It was said that the soldiers were incensed at finding a human scalp — presumably that of an American, taken by some Indian, and sold to the British authorities for the proffered premium—hanging on the wall of the legislative chamber. This scalp and the Speaker's mace were sent to Washington, where the British troops found them when they, in turn, burned our government buildings a little more than a year later.

When Chauncey's fleet left the harbor of York, it sailed due south, and landed the troops at a point four miles east from the mouth of Niagara River, where they went into camp. From here a small expedition was fitted out under Lieutenant Pettigrew, of the navy, who with a hundred men sailed in two schooners to the head of Lake Ontario, to capture a large quantity of stores deposited there. They landed on the 10th of May, drove off the guard, burned the buildings, and brought away the stores. Chauncey himself, with the remainder of the fleet, carried the wounded to Sackett's Harbor, whence he returned on the 25th with provisions, guns, and a reënforcement of about three hundred and fifty men.

General Dearborn immediately planned the capture of Fort George, just above the village of Newark, on the western side of the Niagara, two miles from its mouth. It was arranged that the troops should be landed on the lake shore, and, marching southward and eastward, attack the British works from the land side. The enterprise was admirably planned, and brilliantly executed. The water at the proposed landing-place was carefully sounded, and the stations marked with buoys. A considerable number of boats, to be used in landing the forces, had been built on the shore of the river, were launched on May 26th, and immediately drew the fire of the enemy's batteries.

Before daylight on the morning of the 27th, the fleet weighed anchor. Five of the vessels took positions where they could annoy with a cross-fire the batteries that were within gunshot of the landing-place. · Others took position for the immediate protection of the troops, and at the same time Fort Niagara opened fire on Fort George, which was returned with spirit. All the batteries on the river joined in the contest, and there was a grand chorus of artillery firing. The battery immediately opposite Fort George was the most effective, and considerably damaged that work.

The troops were under the personal command of General Boyd, who had succeeded General Pike. With him were many most skilful and efficient officers, some of whom afterward became famous. The gallant Major Forsyth was there, with his riflemen, and Colonel Macomb with his artillery. Winfield Scott, then a colonel, was there, and Captain Oliver Hazard Perry had hurried down from Lake Erie, to offer his services and take part in the enterprise.

The preparations for the defence had been quite as well made as those for the attack. When the boats loaded with troops approached the shore, a column of two hundred men, posted in a ravine, opened a sharp fire on them. The fire was returned from the boats, which moved on without stopping for a moment or being thrown into any confusion. Captain Hindman, of the artillery, was the first man to land on the enemy's coast; and many of the officers and men were so eager to follow him that they leaped into the water and waded ashore.

The fire of some of the vessels was brought to bear upon the enemy in the ravine ; and as soon as the advance column landed, it formed in battle order and moved forward to the charge.   The enemy soon gave way, but retired slowly, and at the same time a second and stronger column, which had been posted in another ravine, half a mile in the rear, moved forward to protect the retreat of the advance guard and oppose the progress of the Americans.

Every step thus far had been contested, and the roar of cannon and rattle of small arms, both on the water and on shore, had been almost incessant from the beginning of the engagement.   But the blood-iest work was to come.   The combined columns of British troops, numbering eight hundred or more, took a strong position at the top of a steep bank. The advance, under Colonel Scott, moved directly against this position ; but as his men attempted to climb the bank in the face of the enemy, they were mercilessly cut down by a sharp and steady fire. Three times they tried to reach the top, and three times were driven back.   But when Colonel Moses Porter's light artillery and a portion of Boyd's brigade had come up to his assistance, Scott was at length enabled to carry the height.

The victory at this point decided the day. The flying enemy were pursued as far as the village of Newark, at which point Scott detached a force to cut off the retreat westward toward Burlington, while with the remainder of his troops he pressed on at once to Fort George. This work had been so much damaged by the bombardment, and the garrison now left in it was so small, that it was easily captured. As Scott approached it, one of the magazines was exploded, and a heavy stick of timber struck him and knocked him from his horse. Hurrying forward, the soldiers in the advance discovered that trains had been laid for the explosion of two other magazines, and they were just in time to put out the matches. When the gates of the fort were broken open, Scott was the first man to enter, and with his own hands he hauled down the British flag. Close behind him was Colonel Moses Porter, who could not help exclaiming, "Confound your long legs, Scott, you have got in before me!"

A few prisoners were taken with the fort; but Scott, bent upon making his victory complete, made but a brief halt there, and then hurried on his forces in pursuit of the retreating enemy. Twice orders were sent to him to turn back, and both times he refused to obey them. "Your General does not know," said he to a lieutenant who brought one of these orders, "that I have the enemy within my power; in seventy minutes I shall capture his whole force." Colonel Burn, who ranked Scott, but had consented to serve under him, had crossed the river with a troop of cavalry, and was waiting for another now in midstream, to land, when with his whole force he was to join the pursuit. But the fifteen minutes thus lost in waiting enabled General Boyd to ride up in person and peremptorily order the pursuit discontinued, which of course put an end to it. Just why the General did this—whether he feared the victory might be turned into a disaster, or was only apprehensive that Colonel Scott was getting too much glory—has never been explained.

In this action, which was over by noon, the Americans lost one hundred and fifty-three men, killed or wounded. The British loss, as nearly as can be ascertained, was two hundred and seventy-one killed or wounded, and over six hundred unwounded prisoners, five hundred of whom were militia and were paroled.

The British seized the opportunity while Dearborn and his forces were absent on this expedition near the western end of Lake Ontario, to make an attack on Sackett's Harbor, at the eastern. The importance of that place to the Americans consisted mainly in the fact that they had established there a

large depot of naval and military stores, and were
building ships.

The expedition sailed from Kingston in four war-
vessels, a brig, two schooners, and two gunboats, all
under command of Sir James Lucas Yeo. The land
forces, commanded by General Prevost, numbered
about a thousand, besides a party of Indians, said
to have numbered three hundred.

About noon of the 28th the squadron appeared off
Sackett's Harbor, and preparations for landing were
made. But after the troops had been in the boats
about half an hour, an order was issued—for some
mysterious reason, which has never been explained—
commanding them all to return to the ships, which
then stood off for Kingston. But while this was
going on, a fleet of nineteen boats was observed
near the south shore, bringing American reënforcements from Oswego to the Harbor. The Indians,
who thought they were there to fight, and could
not understand why they should return to the ships
without firing a gun, disobeyed the order, and paddled off to attack the Americans in the boats. The
squadron then wore round again, and sent out boat-
loads of troops to the assistance of the Indians, who
drove ashore and captured twelve of the American
boats, after their occupants had escaped to the
woods. The other seven reached the Harbor.

This little affair inspired the British General with new courage, and he resumed the purpose of landing his whole force for an attack on the village.

But meanwhile the Americans were busily preparing for defence. Lieutenant-Colonel Electus Backus, who commanded the remnant of regular troops left at the post, had sent word the evening before to General Jacob Brown, of the militia, who had been requested by General Dearborn to take command in case of an attack during his absence. A militia force numbering about five hundred was hastily gathered from the surrounding country, and added to the small body of regulars and volunteers. The militia were posted behind a ridge of sand which had been thrown up west of the village, where their fire would sweep that part of the shore which offered the only good landing-place for the enemy. On their right were posted the volunteers, with a single piece of artillery. The regulars were formed near their camp about a mile distant.

Early in the morning of the 29th the enemy landed. As their boats approached the shore, the militia and volunteers rose and fired into them, and were fired upon in return by two gunboats that had been sent to cover the landing. The enemy's boats then pulled around to the other side of Horse Island, which is near the mouth of the harbor, landed, and marched steadily across the narrow causeway that connects it with the mainland. As they approached the ridge, the militia gave them another volley, and then fled to the woods, abandoning the piece of artillery. Colonel Mills was killed while trying to hold them to their work. General Brown, who was borne away with the fugitives, succeeded in rallying about eighty of them, whom he posted behind a huge fallen tree, at the edge of a small open field. From this cover they gave the still advancing enemy three or four volleys, and then retreated.

Thus the left of the American line was completely swept away. The right, composed of volunteers, gave way more slowly, and retired in good order along the shore, skirmishing all the way with the enemy's advance, till they reached and formed in line with the regulars. They were annoyed on the way by the enemy's gunboats, which swept portions of the road with grapeshot; but on the other hand the enemy suffered considerably from the fire of their rifles and from parties of regulars sent out by Colonel Backus to join in the skirmishing.

The volunteers took position on the left of the second line of defence. The right was occupied by dismounted light dragoons, and the centre by regular infantry and artillery. The enemy, elated, as he had cause to be, at his first success, came steadily on to attack this line, and as he approached was subjected to an artillery fire from a small work called Fort Tompkins. He struck the right flank of the Americans, but found it made of different stuff from militia. Again and again the attempt was made to force this part of the line ; but the dragoons, commanded by Backus in person, stood firm, delivered their fire with coolness, and drove back the assailants. The fight was kept up for an hour, and at length the weight of numbers told, and the Americans fell back.

A portion of them next took possession of the log barracks, and here made a third stand. The enemy came on as gallantly as ever, intent upon driving everything before him. Colonel Gray, Quarter-master-General, led the red-coats, and as they came up to the attack, an American drummer-boy picked up a musket, levelled it at the Colonel, and shot him down. Lieutenant Fanning, who had been severely wounded at York, and was not-expected to be on duty, took charge of a gun. As the enemy approached, he carefully sighted the piece, and gave them three rounds of grapeshot in quick succession, which broke the force of their onset, and they began to fall back in some disorder. At this moment Colonel Backus fell mortally wounded.

The officer in charge of the stores had been instructed to set fire to them in case the enemy seemed likely to capture the place. Seeing the probability of this, he now applied the torch, not only to the storehouses but also to a new vessel that was almost ready to be launched, and to one that had been recently captured from the enemy.

With the Americans driven to their last stronghold, and the smoke from their burning stores rolling over their heads, the day appeared to be irretrievably lost. But though the enemy was strong in good troops, gallantly led, he had a weak spot in the constitutional timidity of the commander, Sir George Prevost. And General Brown at this point of time made a fortunate movement which struck that weak spot in a most effective way. He had succeeded in rallying about three hundred of the militia, with whom he suddenly emerged from the woods, and made a feint of marching for the boats by which the expedition had landed. Sir George took the alarm at once, imagining he was to be surrounded by a superior force and entrapped. He therefore issued an order for retreat, and his victorious forces withdrew to their ships without securing any result of their victory, or even bearing off their wounded. A reënforcement of six hundred men, under Lieutenant-Colonel Tuttle, who had marched forty miles in one day, reached the village just as the enemy were pushing off in their boats.

The Americans succeeded in putting out the fires, but not till half a million dollars' worth of stores had been destroyed. The new ship was but little injured, as her timbers were so green they would not burn readily. The prize vessel was on fire, and she had considerable powder in her hold; but Lieutenant Talman, at the risk of his life, boarded her, suppressed the flames, and brought her off to a place of safety at a distance from the burning buildings.

Sir George, not content with making a needless fiasco of his expedition, made himself ridiculous by sending a flag of true to demand the surrender of the village and the military post, which of course was refused. He then sent another flag, asking that his dead and wounded might be properly cared for, and on receiving assurances that they would, sailed away with the whole fleet.

The loss of the Americans in this action was about one hundred and seventy, killed, wounded, or missing; that of the British, about two hundred and sixty.

A few days after the loss of Fort George, General Vincent concentrated the British forces at Beaver Dams, and retreated westward to Burlington Bay, the head of Lake Ontario, where he intrenched himself on the heights. General Dearborn, after being baffled for some time by false information which Vincent had caused to be conveyed to him, at length found out where he had gone, and sent the brigades of Winder and Chandler after him. The Americans, following the "ridge road" that skirts the whole shore of the lake, came up with the enemy's pickets at Stony Creek, a small stream that crosses the road at right angles, on the 5th of June. There was considerable skirmishing, and the enemy's pickets were driven in.

General Chandler, with a wise caution thus far seldom displayed, placed a company of artillery at the mouth of the creek, three miles from the road, to cover a landing of boats expected there, with the rest of his forces took a strong position on the high eastern bank of the creek, where the road crosses it, threw out pickets in all directions, gave orders how the line should be formed in case of an attack, and ordered that the artillery horses be kept harnessed.

One regiment at first encamped in the low meadows on the western bank, but after nightfall it withdrew to the heights, leaving its camp-fires burning. A picket guard that had been posted at a little chapel a quarter of a mile in advance was left there.

The officer in command of the enemy's rear guard had sent word to General Vincent that the Americans were in straggling detachments, and if the first were attacked at once it could easily be defeated before the others came up to its support. The General therefore, as he had little chance of further retreat, planned a night attack. A little before midnight of the 5th he left his camp, at the head of about a thousand men, and marched stealthily back by the road he had come, to surprise his foe. The night was absolutely dark, and the sentinels at the little chapel were suddenly seized and silently bayoneted before they could fire their muskets or make any outcry. The assassination of pickets is one of the sickening incidents of war that seldom find mention in the reports of the general or the pages of the romantic historian, but that cost many a poor fellow his life without even the pitiful compensation of what is called glory.

Seeing the camp-fires in the meadow, with no signs of life among them, the British forces imagined that the Americans were all asleep and would fall an easy prey to massacre. They advanced confidently, and as they reached the deserted fires sprang among them with a hideous yell—in which part of the performance they were materially assisted by a few score Indian allies—expecting to see their foes arise from the ground, and rub their eyes open just in time to catch the gleam of the British bayonets and savage tomahawks before they were buried in American flesh.

Instead of this, while they stood dazed among the waning camp-fires, looking about in vain for somebody to massacre, the line on the heights blazed out with musketry and artillery, and the shot tore its way through the ranks of the red-coats. But the English soldier has always been good at obeying orders, and as soon as this volley revealed the whereabouts of the Americans, their enemy pressed on in the face of the fire, climbed the bank, entered the lines in the darkness, and captured several guns, the artillerists not being able to distinguish friend from foe.

Then began a horrible mêlée, in which nearly every man fought on his own account, and many of them could not tell whether they were striking at comrades or enemies. Hearing a few shots fired in the rear of his camp, General Chandler imagined he was attacked from that direction also, and faced about a portion of his line, which increased the dreadful confusion. After this wild work in the darkness and tumult, the British managed somehow to retreat, carrying off with them two pieces of artillery, which, however, were afterward recovered.

When the morning dawned, it was found that the American commanders, Chandler and Winder, were both prisoners in the hands of the enemy ; while the British commander, Vincent, had been thrown from his horse, lost his way in the woods, and after floundering about all night was discovered in a most pitiful and ridiculous plight. Chandler was taken while trying to manœuvre a British regiment, which he had stumbled upon in the darkness and mistaken for one of his own.

In this affair the Americans lost one hundred and fifty-four men, killed, wounded, or missing ; the British, two hundred and fourteen. The victory, so far as there was any, must be accorded to the British, since it broke the advance of the Americans and caused them to turn back. When they had retreated as far as Forty-Mile Creek, they were attacked simultaneously on both flanks — on the land side by a band of Indians, and on the water side by the fleet under Sir James Yeo. But they succeeded in repelling both enemies, and returned to Fort George with the loss only of a part of their baggage, which was conveyed in boats.

After this, Yeo coasted along the shore and captured stores in Charlotte, at the mouth of the Genesee, and in Sodus, on the bay of that name. As he met with some resistance at Sodus, and had difficulty in finding the stores, which were hidden, he burned the buildings there.

There was a British depot of supplies at Beaver Dams, about seven miles southwest of Queenstown and the same distance northwest of the Falls. General Dearborn planned its capture, and on the 23d of June sent against it, from Fort George, an expedition of five hundred and seventy men, commanded by Lieutenant-Colonel Charles G. Bœrstler. The enemy had strong works at Beaver Dams, but at this time they were not very well manned.

The Americans, who had about fifteen miles to march, started in the evening, with the intention of surprising and capturing the post in the morning. But the enemy had been apprised of the movement, and when the Americans reached the present site of Thorold they fell into an ambush, where they were suddenly attacked by four hundred and fifty Indians, commanded by John Brant (son of the celebrated Mohawk chief, Joseph Brant) and Captain Kerr. Though surprised, Bœrstler was not confused. He coolly but quickly formed his men in battle order, and charged through the woods in the direction of the attack. To little purpose, however, as the wily savages, following their usual tactics, fled before the line of bayonets, and soon attacked the Americans from another direction, firing from the thickets and other hiding-places. After keeping up a desultory contest of this sort for three hours, with no prospect of any termination, Bœrstler fell back to a position in an open field, encountering on the way a body of Canadian militia. Scarcely had he taken this new position, to wait for reënforcements which he had asked General Dearborn to send, when a small detachment of British regulars approached to reconnoitre. They were commanded by a Lieutenant Fitzgibbon, who had been warned of the approach of the Americans by a woman who had walked nineteen miles to tell him.

Seeing that his enemy was somewhat disordered, and not disposed to take the offensive, Fitzgibbon, though he had but forty-seven men, conceived the idea of capturing the whole force by one of those tricks which are generally supposed to be peculiarly Yankee. Displaying his little detachment in such a way as to make it appear to be the advance of a much larger body of troops, he sent a flag of truce to Bœrstler and boldly demanded an immediate surrender, saying that fifteen hundred regulars and seven hundred Indians were but a short distance in the rear, and would soon come up. For the truth of this he gave his word, "on the honor of a British soldier." Bœrstler, supposing escape would be impossible, surrendered, on condition that his men should be paroled and permitted to return to the United States. A Major De Haren, who had been sent for in all haste by Fitzgibbon, now came up with two hundred additional troops, and received the surrender, which included five hundred and forty-two men, two guns, and a stand of colors. Major Chapin, who was present, says : '' The articles of capitulation were no sooner signed than they were violated. The Indians immediately commenced their depredations, and plundered the officers of their side arms. The soldiers, too, were stripped of every article of clothing to which the savages took a fancy, such as hats, coats, shoes, etc.'' The British commander also violated the articles by refusing to permit the militia to be paroled, whereupon many of them rose upon the guards, overpowered them, and escaped, taking some of the guards along as prisoners.

This ridiculous affair excited the deepest indignation throughout the country ; and, in obedience to public sentiment, the President soon removed General Dearborn from command.

It was hardly more than a fortnight later, July 11th, when Lieutenant-Colonel Bisshopp planned an attack on Black Rock, a few miles north of Buffalo, where the Americans had a dockyard and large storehouses. With about three hundred men, before daylight of July 11th, he crossed the river in boats, surprised and took possession of the place, and proceeded to burn and plunder as rapidly as possible. He set fire to the block-houses, the barracks, the navy-yard buildings, and a schooner that lay at the wharf, and carried off a considerable quantity of stores. But before he could accomplish all this, General Peter B. Porter had got together a small force, consisting of regulars, volunteers, militia, and a few friendly Indians, and vigorously attacked the invaders. A fight of twenty minutes' duration ended in the precipitate retreat of the British, who left behind them a captain and nine men killed or wounded, and fifteen prisoners. After the boats had pushed off, the Americans renewed their fire, by which Bisshopp, commander of the expedition, was killed, and many of his men were either killed or wounded. The loss of the Americans was three men killed and three wounded. That of the enemy is supposed to have been about seventy. They had carried off four guns, besides spiking all they left. Bisshopp, who had proved himself an energetic and skilful officer, was a serious loss.

Commodore Chauncey, who was a most meritorious naval commander, though he never made a very brilliant reputation, was all this summer trying to bring Sir James Yeo to a decisive battle on Lake Ontario ; but Sir James had a genius for not fighting, and could only be chased to shelter under the guns of the British forts.   It was said also that his instructions forbade his fighting except under the most favorable circumstances.   Once there seemed to be a prospect of a square battle near the mouth of the Niagara, in August ; but Chauncey's plan was frustrated by the captains of two of his schooners, who in disobedience of orders tried to get to windward of the British line, and were captured. On the 28th of September there was a partial engagement between the two squadrons ; but from their unequal sailing, it was only possible to bring three of the American vessels into action.   One of these was badly crippled, but another handled the British flagship so severely that she crowded on all canvas and made off, followed by the entire fleet, which the Americans could not overtake.   On the 5th of October Chauncey gave chase to a squadron which proved to be seven British gunboats used as transports.   One of them was burned, one escaped, and the other five were captured, together with more than two hundred and sixty men.   Two of the prizes were those taken from Chauncey near the Niagara.

These successes left Lake Ontario virtually in the possession of the Americans ; and meanwhile the command of Lake Erie had been gained by a most brilliant and memorable battle.   During the winter of 1812–13 two large brigs, intended to carry twenty guns each, and several gunboats and schooners were built at Presque Isle (now Erie, Pa.), where there was a fine harbor. For this work a force of carpenters was sent from New York. The timber of which they were to construct the vessels was growing in the woods, and the trees had to be felled and worked up at once ; there was no time to wait for the wood to season. All the ironwork, canvas, cordage, and stores had to be brought from New York or Philadelphia, and as there was neither railroad nor canal, and much of the intervening country was a wilderness, the difficulties of transportation were very great. A bar at the mouth of the harbor, on which there was but seven feet of water, prevented the British cruisers from sailing in and destroying the vessels before they were launched.

Captain Oliver Hazard Perry, who, though quite young, had seen considerable service afloat, was ordered from the seaboard to take command on Lake Erie, and arrived at Buffalo in March. His volunteer service in the attack on Fort George has been already mentioned. The fall of that work was followed by the abandonment of Fort Erie, which released the vessels that had been blockaded by its guns in the upper part of the Niagara, and early in June they rendezvoused at Presque Isle.

Perry now had his entire force in one harbor, and pushed on his equipment with the greatest possible speed.   One of the new brigs was made his flagship, and was named the *Lawrence.*   The bar that had thus far protected the fleet was now a hindrance to its sailing, for it could be passed by the larger vessels only in calm weather, and even then they must be lightened of their guns and heavy stores.   The British commander, Captain R. H. Barclay, was watching with his entire fleet for Perry to come out. If, as is supposed, he intended to attack him while crossing the bar, when he could probably have won a victory, he lost his opportunity by attending to pleasure before duty.   A gentleman living on the northern shore of the lake invited him to dinner one Sunday, and he crossed over with his whole squadron.   At the same time the water became smooth, and Perry, who had been eagerly watching for such a chance, proceeded to take out his fleet at once.

The *Lawrence,* which was his heaviest vessel, was provided with a large scow on each side, and on her arrival at the bar these scows were nearly filled with water, and sunk very low.   Great beams were then passed through her port-holes, the ends projecting over the scows.   Piles of blocks were provided for these ends to rest upon, and then the holes in the scows were plugged up, and the water pumped out.

As the scows rose, they lifted the brig with them. But though her guns had been taken out and left on the beach, as well as all other heavy articles that could be removed, she still drew too much water to pass the bar. Another lift was made, which occupied the night, and finally she floated across. The other brig, the *Niagara*, was not quite so large, and was taken over with less difficulty. The lighter vessels had crossed the bar without assistance ; and on the approach of the English squadron at eight o'clock the next morning, it was received with a cannonade, which, though it did no harm, prevented Barclay from running in close and seizing the prey he had been so long watching for. The *Lawrence's* guns were taken on board as soon as she was afloat outside, and the broadside was trained to bear on the enemy.

This was Monday, the 5th of August, and Perry was now afloat on Lake Erie with ten vessels, carrying fifty-five guns and—after he had received several reënforcements—about four hundred. men. Captain Barclay had about the same number of men, in six vessels, carrying sixty-five guns, his flagship being the *Detroit*. As soon as the American fleet was fairly over the bar, the British sailed away up the lake, and it took Perry a month to find them and bring them to action. He was at Put-in-Bay, in one of the islands near the western end of the lake, when at sunrise on the morning of September 10th the British fleet was sighted from the masthead, bearing down from the northwest, apparently bent on having a fight.

Perry had given the commanders of his several vessels careful instructions what to do in case of an engagement, ending with the remark that " they could not be out of their proper places if they laid their enemy close alongside." Within an hour after the enemy was sighted, the squadron was beating out of the bay. The wind was from the southwest, which made it impossible for the Americans to get the weather-gage, unless by circumnavigating some of the islands. As there was apparently no time for this, Perry determined to accept the chances of battle without that advantage, and accordingly passed to leeward of the islands. But fortune favored him unexpectedly, for the wind soon shifted to the southeast, giving him the weather-gage, which for vessels armed as his were was very important.

At ten o'clock the British squadron, having failed in manœuvres for the weather-gage, hove to, in line of battle, with their bows to the west and south, and awaited the approach of their enemy, now about nine miles distant. One of the smaller vessels was at the head of the line, and the *Detroit*, Barclay's flagship, next ; then came another small vessel, and then the *Queen Charlotte*, a large one, and then the two remaining small ones. The British vessels were all freshly painted, and had new canvas, presenting a handsome appearance to the eye of a sailor.

As Perry approached and observed this order, he formed his own line to correspond with it. He placed two schooners in the van, one carrying four guns and the other two ; then his flagship, the *Lawrence ;* then the *Caledonia*, of three guns ; then the *Niagara*, of twenty ; and then the other vessels, which, however, as the wind was light, did not come up very promptly. The orders were, that the vessels should be but half a cable's length apart.

As he approached the enemy, Perry displayed a blue flag bearing the words, " Don't give up the ship."* A few minutes before twelve o'clock, a bugle was sounded on the British flagship, which was answered by cheers from all the other vessels in the line, and followed by the discharge of one of her long guns, pointed at the *Lawrence*. As the American was still a mile and a half distant, the shot fell short ; but this space was being gradually lessened, and the battle was soon fairly opened. One of the two schooners in the van replied with a

---

* For the origin of this motto, see page 199.

long gun, while the *Lawrence*, being armed with carronades, bore down upon the British flagship, to engage her at short range. This she succeeded in doing, but not without suffering considerably, and the three largest of the British vessels concentrated their fire on her. The two foremost schooners fought their long guns well ; but as they had been ordered to keep to windward of the flagship (that is, a little farther from the enemy) they did not draw off any of the fire from her. But, after two hours of this, the *Niagara* drew ahead of the *Caledonia*, thus assuming the place in the line next to the *Lawrence*, and fought most gallantly ; still, this hardly lessened the fire that was poured into the flagship, which the enemy seemed determined to sink. Many of her spars were shot away, all of her guns on the starboard side, but one, were rendered useless, and of a hundred men on board, twenty-two were killed and sixty-one wounded—a proportion of casualties that had never been equalled in any similar battle.

The *Lawrence* dropped out of the fight, and Perry transferred his flag to the *Niagara*, which pulled ahead to a position for engaging the *Detroit*. When the enemy saw the flag come down, they supposed they had gained a victory, stopped firing, and cheered. But the decisive struggle was yet to come. Captain Elliott, of the *Niagara*, passed down the line in a small boat, delivering to the commander of each vessel Perry's order to close up and attack the enemy at half pistol-shot with grape and canister. He then remained with and commanded one of the last vessels in the line, leaving the *Niagara* to Perry. .

At this time the wind freshened, Perry showed the signal for close action, an answering cheer passed along his line, and once more the whole squadron bore down upon the enemy. Barclay attempted to manœuvre his vessels so as to bring his uninjured broadsides to bear ; but his line got into confusion, and two of the vessels fouled.

Perry took prompt advantage of this. The *Niagara* sailed right through the confused British line, having two of their vessels on one side, and three on the other—all within short range—and delivered her deadly broadsides in both directions as she passed. Then she luffed across their bows, and raked them, and the cries that came from the *Detroit* told that this merciless operation had had its usual deadly effect. At the same time, the other American vessels came into close action, and their guns were served with great rapidity. This destructive work had lasted about twenty minutes when an officer of the *Queen Charlotte* displayed a white handkerchief on the point of a pike, and four of the

British vessels struck their colors. The other two
attempted to escape, but were overtaken in about
an hour and compelled to surrender.

In this battle, the entire loss of the Americans
was twenty-seven killed and ninety-six wounded.
Twelve of these were quarterdeck officers. As
more than a hundred out of four hundred on board
had previously been rendered unfit for duty by
dysentery and cholera, the proportion of casualties
to effective men was more than one in three. The
British lost forty-one killed and ninety-four wounded, including twelve officers. Captain Barclay, who
had lost his left arm in a previous engagement, in
this one lost the use of his right.

The masts of the *Detroit* and *Queen Charlotte* were
so injured that they snapped off two days later,
from the rolling of the vessels in the bay, while riding at anchor during a gale.

In a despatch to General Harrison, Perry announced his victory in words that have become
famous : '' We have met the enemy, and they are
ours : two ships, two brigs, one schooner, and one
sloop.'' Congress voted him a gold medal for his
achievement. As the question of the fighting qual-
ities of the black man has since been considerably
discussed, it is worth noting that in this bloody and
brilliant battle a large number of Perry's men were

Negroes.   Much of the credit of the victory has been claimed for Captain Jesse D. Elliott, who undoubtedly deserved it, and his services were generously acknowledged in Perry's official report.

Many interesting incidents of this famous action have been related by different participants.   At the opening of the battle, the English musicians played the well-known air of " Rule, Britannia !—Britannia, rule the waves !"—on which the result of the fight was a ludicrous comment, proving that an exception must be made in favor of the waves of Lake Erie.

On the British flagship there was a pet bear, and when the victors stepped on board they found it eagerly lapping up the blood from the deck.

The British commander had repeated the silly performance of nailing his colors to the mast, which never has any other effect than to sacrifice lives that might have been saved if the signal of surrender, when surrender became necessary, could have been displayed instantly.

On Captain Barclay's vessel were three Indians, whom he placed in the tops, or cross-trees, with rifles in their hands, to pick off the American officers, that kind of work being exactly suited to their taste.   But as the first part of the action was fought at long cannon-range, beyond the reach of rifle-shot, they found themselves in danger from numerous large balls that went tearing through the rigging, and at the same time totally unable to murder anybody on the distant vessels. Indians have always stood in mortal terror of artillery. So they descended to the deck ; but here they found it still more dangerous, and finally the disgusted braves retreated down the hatchway. When the Americans came on board, they found them hidden in the hold. This is probably the only instance of Indians taking part, or attempting to take part, in modern naval warfare. But they have a legend of a great Indian naval battle that took place on the waters of this same lake two hundred years before.

The Senecas—so runs the story—who inhabited the southern and eastern shores of Ontario and the St. Lawrence, had declared war against the Wyandots, who inhabited the northern and western shores. A Wyandot chief, gambling with a Seneca, had won his wife ; but the Seneca refused to give her up. Shortly afterward she eloped with the Wyandot, and they escaped to the country of the Pottawatomies, in Michigan. This was the cause of the war, which the Senecas began by crossing the St. Lawrence, surprising a Wyandot village, and cruelly murdering a large number of the inhabitants.

Finally the whole Wyandot nation fled before their enemies, passed along the northern shore of Lake

Ontario, crossed the peninsula north of Lake Erie, and after great suffering and serious losses escaped by crossing St. Clair River on cakes of floating ice.

The next summer the Senecas planned a naval expedition against the Wyandots, to be fitted out at the eastern end of Lake Erie, near the present site of Buffalo, pass up the lake and through Detroit River, and rescue the stolen squaw and exterminate the tribe. But the Wyandots had early information of this design, and several of the tribes inhabiting the peninsula of Michigan joined with them in preparations to repel the threatened invasion.

The war-canoes built by the Senecas were "dug-outs," hewn from the trunks of large trees. The Wyandots and their allies prepared a fleet of birch-bark canoes, which were much lighter, swifter, and more easily manœuvred, and went down the lake to meet their enemy. They coasted along the northern shore as far as North Point, where they waited to make a reconnoissance. The Wyandot who had carried off the woman crossed the lake alone, climbed a tall tree overlooking the rendezvous of the Senecas, and counted their craft and noted their preparations. Then he passed by a wide circuit around their encampment, swam the Niagara below the Falls, and the next day rejoined the fleet of the allies, to whom he was able to give all necessary information as to the number and equipment of their enemy.

They set sail—or rather pulled paddles—at once. But when in full sight of the Senecas, pretended to be frightened, and retreated. The Senecas gave a war-whoop, launched their heavy canoes, and paddled after them as fast as possible. When the allies had thus drawn their antagonists far away from the shore, they suddenly turned upon them, and a bloody and merciless battle ensued, which lasted for several hours. Indian after Indian was cut down, or gradually hacked to pieces, or knocked overboard. Some of the canoes were run down; others were grappled together while their occupants fought hand-to-hand. The lighter boats of the allies were a great advantage, and finally the Senecas were defeated. The dead and the badly wounded were then thrown overboard, while the prisoners were reserved for torture. One Seneca was found to have concealed himself in the bottom of a canoe, feigning death that he might escape captivity. The victors cut off his nose and ears, and knocked out his teeth, and in that disgraceful plight sent him home to bear the news of the disaster to his tribe. On the bank of Niagara River the captured canoes were piled up for a funeral pyre, and a hundred of the wounded Senecas were tied and laid upon it. Fire was set to it, and as one and another escaped when his shackles were burned off, he was shot down with arrows or brained with a war-club. When the victims were all reduced to ashes, the allies celebrated their victory with a feast and dance, and then returned home. Such was the legend told by Walk-in-the-Water, a Wyandot chief, when he heard of Perry's victory, which he thought was a small affair in comparison with the exploit of his ancestors.

By the capture of the British fleet, the lakes were cleared of the enemy, and but one more movement was necessary in order to restore to the United States all that had been lost by Hull's surrender. How successfully that movement was executed will be shown in the next chapter.

CHAPTER VIII.

BATTLE OF THE THAMES.

Harrison's Advance—Proctor's Retreat—Nature of the Ground—Disposition of the Indians—The Battle—Death of Tecumseh—Flight of Proctor—Results of the Campaign.

THE opportunity which General Harrison had been waiting for had now arrived. He had been joined by Governor Shelby, of Kentucky, who brought three thousand five hundred mounted men, and also by two hundred Indians. His preparations for an invasion of Canada were complete ; and Perry's victory not only gave him the necessary means of transportation, but removed a hostile fleet that might have prevented his landing an army on Canadian soil. His troops rendezvoused on the peninsula near Sandusky ; the total force, including a few regulars, numbering about five thousand men.

Colonel Richard M. Johnson, with his regiment of cavalry, was sent to Detroit by land, there to cross the river. All the other troops, with their equipments, were taken on board Perry's vessels and carried up Detroit River, and landed, on the 27th of September, at a point three miles below Amherstburg. They marched at once on Malden, and took possession of that post without opposition. The British General Proctor had abandoned it, but not till he had destroyed the barracks, the stores, and as much of the fortifications as was possible. Harrison expected a fight, and had his forces formed in battle order as they advanced ; but Proctor's purpose was simply to get out of the way of his enemy, and escape if possible to Niagara. He had about six hundred white soldiers who were fit for duty, and a force of Indians variously estimated at from eight hundred to fifteen hundred.

Harrison left detachments at Detroit, Amherstburg, and Sandwich, and with the remainder of his force—about three thousand five hundred men—set out, on the 2d of October, in pursuit of Proctor. The enemy had retreated along the southern shore of Lake St. Clair, and thence up the river Thames, which flows into that lake. Proctor's baggage and artillery were carried by water, in small vessels ; and Harrison in his pursuit was materially aided by Captain Perry, whose boats carried the baggage and supplies the whole length of the lake and fifteen miles up the river. At that point Perry left the water, and served on Harrison's staff.

Four considerable streams crossed the line of retreat, and Proctor might have seriously delayed the pursuit, and perhaps entirely stopped it, by destroying the bridge over any one of them. He seems not to have thought of this at the first stream, where the Americans found the bridge intact. At the second, a lieutenant and eleven men had been left with orders to destroy the bridge ; but before they had accomplished their task, Harrison's advance guard came up and captured them. The third bridge, partially destroyed, was defended by a considerable body of Indians ; but a few shots from two six-pounders dispersed them, and the structure was soon repaired. The fourth bridge was likewise partly destroyed, and guarded by Indians, who were not so easily driven away. The mounted Kentuckians pushed forward, and had a brisk skirmish with the savages, in which half a dozen of the whites were killed or wounded, and thirteen of the Indians were killed. The enemy then set fire to a large house near the bridge, a distillery, and three vessels that were loaded with military stores, and continued his retreat. As soon as the bridge could be repaired, Harrison's troops crossed it, extinguished the fire in the house, and found in it two thousand stand of arms. Early on the 5th the pursuit was renewed. The route was still along the Thames, and in the course of the day the Americans captured two gun-boats and several batteaux, all laden with provisions and ammunition.

By this time, Proctor's Indians were tired of retreating, and were determined either to have a fight
of some sort or leave him. About sixty of them
actually deserted, and offered their services to Harrison, who declined them—not because he disbelieved in the employment of Indians, for he had
some in his own force, but probably because he
thought it unwise to employ troops of any sort who
recognized no principle and were ready to go from
one side to the other as the fortunes of war might
fluctuate.

Both armies were now on the north side of the
Thames, and Harrison's scouts brought news that
the enemy had formed in line of battle at a point
about two and a half miles from Moravian Town,
four miles in advance of where Harrison then was.
At the place chosen there was a marsh, the edge of
which was about five hundred yards distant from
the river and parallel with it for two miles. Midway between was a little marsh. The road ran between the little marsh and the river. The ground
was largely covered with an open growth of forest
trees, but there was no underbrush.

Proctor placed his best English troops, with his
artillery, in a line stretching from the river to the
little marsh, his cannon commanding the road. Behind this line were his reserves. The Indians, com-

manded by Tecumseh, who was a brigadier-general in the British service, formed a line between the two marshes, and a large number of them were thrown forward in the edge of the great marsh, that they might fall upon the left flank of the Americans.

Harrison placed his mounted troops in front, and behind them two thirds of his infantry, while the remainder was thrown back at an angle on the left, to be able to face the Indians in the marsh. The mounted men were formed in two columns, all under command of Colonel Richard M. Johnson, who rode with the left column. The right column was commanded immediately by his brother, Lieutenant-Colonel James Johnson.

At the sound of the bugle, the columns rode forward, slowly and steadily at first. As the right column came within musket-shot of the enemy, it received a volley or two, and here and there a trooper tumbled from his horse. The pace was immediately quickened, and in two minutes a solid column of a thousand dragoons went crashing through the British line, cutting down every opposing soldier within reach of its sabres. The column immediately re-formed in rear of the enemy's position, and repeated the charge, at the same time firing into the broken ranks, when the entire left wing was thrown into confusion before the men could fix their bayonets, and four hundred and seventy of them, with their officers, surrendered.

On the other wing, as Colonel Richard M. Johnson's column rode up at a charge, the Indians reserved their fire till they were within a few paces, and then gave them a destructive volley. Almost the whole of the advance guard fell before it, and Colonel Johnson was wounded. Finding that the ground here, between the two marshes, was unsuitable for horses, Colonel Johnson at once ordered his men to dismount, and for eight or ten minutes there was hard fighting, at close range, with the rifle. After charges and counter-charges, the Indians began to give way. At this moment Governor Shelby brought up the reserves, and about the same time Tecumseh fell, and the savages then broke and fled.

The question, who killed Tecumseh, though not of much importance, has been warmly discussed. Thomson, one of the earliest authorities for the history of this war, says : " Colonel R. M. Johnson had been five times wounded, and in that state, covered with blood, and exhausted by pain and fatigue, he personally encountered Tecumseh. The Colonel was mounted on a white charger, at which, being a conspicuous object, the Indians had continually levelled their fire. A shower of bullets had fallen round him ; his holsters, his clothes, and most of his accoutrements were pierced in several places ; and at the instant when he discovered Tecumseh, his horse received a second wound. Tecumseh, having discharged his rifle, sprang forward with his tomahawk, and had it already raised to throw, when Colonel Johnson's horse staggered back, and immediately the Colonel drew forth a pistol, shot the Indian through the head, and both fell to the ground together.''

When the savages in front were defeated, those that had been posted in the edge of the great marsh vanished through the woods.

General Proctor, when he saw his lines broken, abandoned the field and drove off with all possible speed in his carriage, accompanied by a mounted body guard. He was conscious that he deserved no quarter for his cold-blooded massacres, and feared that if he fell into the hands of American soldiers he might get his deserts. As a matter of fact, General Harrison had instructed his men before the battle that if Proctor was captured he should be brought in unharmed. A detachment sent in pursuit of him pressed him so closely that he abandoned his carriage, leaving his sword and private papers in it, and took to the woods ; where, as he was well mounted and familiar with the country, they could not overtake him. But though he escaped the

Americans, by his own government he was court-martialled, reprimanded, and suspended for six months. If he had previously been punished for violating the laws of war, and an abler and better man put into his place, this disaster might not have befallen the British arms. It was not when they massacred defenceless people, but only when they lost battles, that the English Government was dissatisfied with unsoldier-like conduct in its officers.

In this action, the Americans lost about fifty men killed or wounded. Among the killed was Colonel Whitley, a soldier of the Revolution, who had volunteered as a private. The British lost about a hundred and eighty killed or wounded, and nearly all the remainder were made prisoners. It was supposed that about a hundred and twenty Indians were killed ; at least thirty-three were left dead on the field, and an unknown number carried away. Among the spoils of the victory were several brass cannon which had been captured with Burgoyne at Saratoga, surrendered by Hull at Detroit, and now came a second time into the hands of the Americans.

Harrison destroyed Moravian Town the day after the battle, and then marched back to Detroit. Proctor had the good taste to send a flag of truce, requesting that the prisoners be humanely treated. As General Harrison had already given up his own tent to some of the wounded British officers, it is probable that they were.

By this brief and brilliant campaign, Harrison destroyed the British power in that part of Canada, restored the territory of Michigan to the United States, killed the great Indian leader who had been the most dangerous enemy of the Americans in the West, separated the tribes that had been assisting the English, and compelled some of them to make peace on his own terms. At Detroit he discharged Shelby's volunteers, gave the place a garrison of a thousand men, restored civil law, and made General Cass provisional governor of the territory. Three weeks later, he and the remainder of his troops were taken on board Perry's fleet and carried to Buffalo.

On the same day that the battle of the Thames was fought, Commodore Chauncey, in pursuit of Yeo's fleet on Lake Ontario, captured a cutter and four transports, on board of which were two hundred and sixty-four British officers and soldiers.

CHAPTER IX.

WILKINSON'S EXPEDITION.

Armstrong's Plans—Position of the Troops—Descent of the St. Lawrence—Battle of Chrysler's Field—Hampton's Defeat—Cost of the Campaign—Effects on the Niagara Frontier—Capture of Fort Niagara—Destruction of Buffalo and other Villages.

THE final military operations of this year on the northern border were the most disappointing, and on the whole the most disgraceful, of any that had been undertaken. General John Armstrong had become Secretary of War early in the year, and in February had submitted a plan, which the President at once approved, for the conquest of Canada by means of an expedition against Montreal.

Armstrong had seen service in the Revolution, and was the author of the anonymous "Newburg Addresses," which had given Washington so much trouble. Although he planned the expedition in February, he allowed the entire summer to go by before attempting its execution, and it set out in October, the worst time of year for such an undertaking. The first requisite for any military movement is, that it shall be under the supreme command of some one man. But the left wing of the army which was to make this one was commanded by General James Wilkinson, at Sackett's Harbor, while the right wing was under General Wade Hampton, at Plattsburg, and between these two officers there was not only no cordial friendship, but a positive jealousy that rendered it almost impossible for them to act in concert. Although Wilkinson was the ranking officer, Hampton maintained that his own must be considered as a separate and independent command, and himself not subordinate to anybody but the Secretary of War. He thus put in practice on a small scale a vicious principle whose advocacy on a vastly larger scale has since given some of his descendants an unenviable prominence.

So old a soldier as Armstrong should have known that the first thing necessary to the success of his scheme was the removal of one or the other of these officers, and conferring upon some one general the absolute command of all forces that were to take part in it. As he had stationed himself and his War Department at Sackett's Harbor, he perhaps imagined that he could direct the expedition from there, and, holding both generals subordinate to himself, cause the two wings to act in concert. If so, he was wofully mistaken. A man sixty years of age, who owned three thousand slaves and was accustomed to no check upon his least caprice, who

now had four thousand troops under his command
—a large number in that war—and was distant a
hundred and fifty miles from his superior, with a
wilderness between, could not be expected to hold
himself subordinate to anybody.

General Wilkinson had removed most of the
troops from Fort George on the Niagara, taking
them down the lake, and he now had a total force
of about eight thousand men. The right wing, under Hampton, numbered half as many more. The
final plan was, to move down the St. Lawrence with
Wilkinson's force, while Hampton's moved northward to unite with it at or near the mouth of the
Chateaugua ; the combined force then to strike for
Montreal. Wilkinson rendezvoused his troops at
Grenadier Island, eighteen miles below Sackett's
Harbor, near the point where the waters of the lake
find their outlet in the St. Lawrence. The British
were apprised of the movement, and drew a large
force from the Niagara frontier to Kingston, supposing that was to be the point of attack ; and indeed this had been the first intention of the Americans. To strengthen this impression on the part of
the enemy, and induce him to hold his forces at
Kingston as long as possible, Wilkinson appointed a
second rendezvous at the mouth of French Creek,
eighteen miles farther down. The command of the

advance was given to General Jacob Brown, who had successfully defended Sackett's Harbor in May. On the 1st and 2d of November the British squadron attacked the advance, but without effecting anything.

On the 5th Wilkinson's entire force moved down the St. Lawrence. They occupied more than three hundred boats, which made a procession five miles long. At Prescott the river was commanded by British batteries, and to avoid them Wilkinson debarked his troops and stores a short distance above that place, and sent them by land to Red Mill, some distance below. The boats were run by the batteries at night, and escaped injury, though under a heavy fire for a considerable time.

But it was found that the enemy had planted batteries at several other places, to obstruct and if possible destroy the flotilla. Colonel Alexander Macomb was ordered to cross the river with twelve hundred of the best troops in the army, and, marching down the north bank, abreast of the flotilla, drive away or capture the gunners. In this task he was assisted by Forsyth's riflemen, who crossed a little later. The cavalry and Brown's brigade passed over next day.

They found plenty of fighting to do, though of a desultory kind. There was a battery at nearly every narrow place in the river, and small parties of the enemy were continually hanging on the rear of the Americans, firing whenever they found a chance. Eight miles below Hamilton, Macomb had a fight with a party strongly posted in a block-house, and succeeded in driving them out.

. Meanwhile General De Rottenburg, who had come down to Kingston from Queenstown, sent a force of fifteen hundred men, with two schooners and seven gunboats, to follow the expedition and attack its rear guard at every opportunity. It was Commodore Chauncey's duty to prevent any British force from leaving the harbor of Kingston at this time ; but unaccountably he failed to do it. On the 9th the American riflemen had a brisk skirmish with a body of Canadian militia and Indians, and finally drove them off.

By the 10th the Long Rapid was reached, and Wilkinson put most of his men ashore, that the boats might shoot the rapid with greater safety. That evening the British gun-boats came up and opened a cannonade upon the barges, which for a time threatened to destroy them. But the Americans took two eighteen-pounders ashore, and improvised a battery, with which they soon drove off the gun-boats.

By this time the enemy's forces were pretty well

united in the rear of the expedition, and the gun-boats had been brought to act in concert. It was evident that the Americans could not safely proceed farther till a battle had been fought.

The troops were encamped on the farm of John Chrysler, a captain in the British service, a short distance below Williamsburg. On the morning of the 11th it was found that the enemy had taken a position close in the rear, in battle order, his left resting on a swamp, and his right on the river, where his gun-boats were moored. His line was well placed, and he had three pieces of artillery in position. As General Wilkinson was too ill to take the field, or even rise from his bed, the command of the American forces devolved upon General John Parker Boyd. Boyd, now about fifty years of age, had entered the United States service as early as 1786, but later had been a soldier of fortune in India, raising and equipping there, at his own expense, a force of fifteen hundred men, and selling their services to the highest bidder. Still later he returned to the United States, and was with Harrison at the battle of Tippecanoe.

Orders were given to drive back the enemy, and General Robert Swartwout's brigade dashed into the woods and routed the British advance, which fell back upon the main body. The brigade of General

Leonard Covington supported Swartwout's, attacking the British right while Swartwout attacked the left. It was a cold, raw day, and part of the time there was snow and sleet in the air. There were charges and counter-charges, the contending columns alternately advancing and retiring across ploughed fields, where the men were often up to their knees in mud. All the romance of war was lacking, while all its disagreeable elements were present in full force. There were wounds enough, and death enough, and misery enough, and, as it proved, no decisive or profitable victory for either side. The Americans had the greater number of men, but this advantage was fully counterbalanced by the fact that they were the attacking party, and there were several deep ravines which they could not cross with their artillery to bring it into use, while the British used their own guns throughout the action.

The attack was spirited and determined, and seemed likely to succeed ; but after a while the American right wing found its ammunition exhausted, and about the same time the left was discouraged and thrown into some confusion by the fall of General Covington, mortally wounded. The enemy now massed troops on his right wing, and pressed forward heavily, so that he captured one of the American guns ; a charge of cavalry under Adjutant-

General Walbach, and the coolness and bravery of Captain Armstrong Irvine, being all that prevented him from seizing the others.

For two hours longer the contest swayed to and fro across the miry fields for the distance of a mile, till the Americans brought up a reserve of six hundred men under Lieutenant-Colonel Upham, by which order was restored and the line firmly established, to await the next onset of the enemy. But no further assault was made, and in the night the Americans retired unmolested to their boats.

This action is sometimes called the battle of Williamsburg, sometimes the battle of Chrysler's Field. Both sides claimed the victory, and there has been much dispute both as to the number of men engaged and as to the losses. The British probably had a thousand men, including Indians ; the Americans seventeen hundred. General Wilkinson reported a loss of one hundred and two killed, and two hundred and thirty-seven wounded—one man in five. The British loss was reported at one hundred and eighty-eight killed, wounded, or missing—nearly one in five. Among the American officers who distinguished themselves on this field was Lieutenant William J. Worth, who afterward rose to eminence as a major-general.

Disregarding the military maxim which forbids an

invading army to leave an enemy in its rear, Wilkinson next day passed down the Long Rapids with his whole force, and near Cornwall was joined by General Brown, who had been sent forward to attack the post at the foot of the rapids. This had been done by a fight at Hoophole Creek, where about eight hundred of Brown's men, under the immediate command of Colonel Scott, had defeated an equal number of the enemy and taken many prisoners.

But here a courier arrived at Wilkinson's headquarters, bringing a letter from General Hampton, in which he announced that he would not join the expedition as ordered, or attempt to invade Canada any farther.

The truth was, Hampton had moved down the Chateaugua with about four thousand men, intending to join Wilkinson. He was opposed by a force of about one thousand, including Indians, commanded by Lieutenant-Colonel De Salaberry. The active opposition began at a point where the road passed through a forest. Here the enemy had felled trees across the line of march, constructed abattis, and posted light troops and Indians in the woods. But Hampton sent a regiment to turn the enemy's flank and occupy the open country in the rear, while strong working parties opened a new road by a detour, enabling his whole force to follow, and thus the first obstruction was skilfully passed.

But eight or ten miles in advance a more formidable obstacle was encountered. Here was another forest, in which the enemy had constructed not only abattis but timber breastworks, and planted artillery. The guides assured Hampton that the river, along whose bank his route lay, was fordable opposite the enemy's flank. He thereupon formed an elaborate plan for sending a force to ford the stream above, march to a point below the enemy, ford again, and fall on his flank and rear ; while the main body was to attack in front when the firing was heard. The detachment was commanded by Colonel Purdy, who afterward said it " was intrusted to the guidance of men, each of whom repeatedly assured him [Hampton] that they were not acquainted with the country, and were not competent to direct such an expedition ; while at the same time he had a man who had a perfect knowledge of the country, whom he promised to send, but which he neglected to do."

The detachment, which left camp in the evening of October 25th, crossed the stream, and soon got lost in a hemlock swamp, where it wandered about in the darkness, sometimes doubling on its tracks, so that the two ends of the column would come in contact with each other and wonder whether they had met friend or foe. As might have been expected, it completely failed to find the lower ford.

In the afternoon of the 26th, though nothing had been heard from the detachment, the main force moved against the works in front. De Salaberry boldly threw forward a force to meet it, resting his left on the river and his right on a thick wood, in the edge of which' he posted a body of Indians. The cracking of rifles began at once, and sharp and persistent fighting ensued. Slowly and steadily the Americans, under the immediate command of General George Izard, pressed back this advance upon the main body of the enemy. But at this point the detachment across the river encountered a detachment of British troops. Purdy's advance guard was driven back, and then fire was opened upon him by a concealed body of militia, which threw him into confusion and caused a disorderly retreat. At the same time, Hampton was deceived by a ruse of De Salaberry's, who had placed buglers at several points in the woods, with orders to sound an advance. Thoroughly disconcerted, and perhaps frightened by this failure of his plan, and the supposed onset of a great force of the enemy, Hampton at once withdrew his troops and abandoned the attack, falling back soon afterward to Chateaugua Four Corners.

He had lost about forty men killed or wounded ; the enemy about twenty-five.

On learning of the defection of Hampton, Wilkinson called a council of war, the result of which was a determination to ascend Salmon River and go into winter quarters.   Thus ended ingloriously one more of the ill-advised and ill-managed attempts to conquer Lower Canada.

The cost of these campaigns had been enormous to both belligerents.   The Americans had spent about two and a half million dollars in building vessels on lakes Erie, Ontario, and Champlain ; which was a large sum for that day, and yet was small in comparison with the incidental cost of maintaining considerable bodies of troops in idleness through a whole summer while waiting for the fleets to be built.   It was estimated that the conveyance of each cannon to Sackett's Harbor had cost a thousand dollars.   The flour for Harrison's army, by the time it reached the troops, had cost a hundred dollars a barrel.   There were long distances through the wilderness of Western New York and Northern Ohio where supplies could only be carried on packhorses, half a barrel to a horse, and other horses had to follow with forage for those that were carrying the supplies.   Most of the horses were used up by a single trip.   Of four thousand used in carrying provisions to Harrison, but eight hundred were alive the next spring. In Canada the hardships of war rested heavily upon the people as well as the soldiers. All their salt had come from the United States, and what little there was on that side of the border when communication with this country ceased was held at a dollar a quart. At Kingston flour was thirty dollars a barrel. So scarce were provisions of all kinds, that the Government appointed commissioners to determine how much food each family should be permitted to consume. In the British camps, lean cattle were killed to prevent their starving to death, and then the meat was eaten by the soldiers. In later wars we have often succeeded in shooting more men, but seldom in producing more misery.

The withdrawal of troops from the Niagara frontier to take part in Wilkinson's expedition left the defence of that line almost entirely to militia, and the term for which the militia had been called out expired on the 9th of December. The next day General George McClure, who had been left in command at Fort George, found himself at the head of but sixty effective men, while the British General Drummond had brought up to the peninsula four hundred troops and seventy Indians—released by the failure of Wilkinson's expedition—and was preparing to attack him.

McClure thereupon determined to evacuate the fort, as the only alternative from capture or destruction, and remove his men and stores across the river to Fort Niagara. He also determined to burn the village of Newark, that the enemy might find no shelter. The laudable part of this plan was but imperfectly carried out ; he failed to destroy the barracks, and left unharmed tents for fifteen hundred men, several pieces of artillery, and a large quantity of ammunition, all of which fell into the hands of Drummond's men. But the inexcusable part—the burning of a village in midwinter, inhabited by non-combatants who had been guilty of no special offence—was only too faithfully executed. The inhabitants were given twelve hours in which to remove their goods, and then the torch was applied, and not a house was left standing.

This needless cruelty produced its natural result ; Drummond determined upon swift and ample retaliation. In the night of December 18th, just one week after the burning of Newark, he threw across the Niagara a force of five hundred and fifty men. They landed at Five Mile Meadows, three miles above Fort Niagara, and marched upon it at once, arriving there at four o'clock in the morning. McClure, who had received an intimation of the enemy's intention to devastate the American frontier, had gone to Buffalo to raise a force to oppose him. The garrison of the fort consisted of about four hundred and fifty men, a large number of whom were in the hospital. The command had been left to a Captain Leonard, who at this time was three miles away, sleeping at a farm-house.

The most elaborate preparations had been made for the capture of the fort, including scaling-ladders · for mounting the bastions. But the Americans seemed to have studied to make the task as easy as possible. The sentries were seized and silenced before they could give any alarm, and the main gate was found standing wide open, so that the British had only to walk straight in and begin at once the stabbing which had been determined upon.

The guard in the south-east block-house fired one volley, by which the British commander, Colonel Murray, was wounded, and a portion of the invalids made what resistance they could. A British lieu- tenant and five men were killed, and a surgeon and three men wounded. Sixty-five Americans, two thirds of whom were invalids, were bayoneted in their beds ; fifteen others, who had taken refuge in the cellars, were despatched in the same manner, and fourteen were wounded ; twenty escaped, and all the others, about three hundred and forty, were made prisoners. Some accounts say also that the women in the fort were treated with great cruelty and indignity.

On the same morning, General Riall, with a detachment of British troops and five hundred Indians, crossed from Queenstown and attacked Lewiston. The small force of Americans here, under Major Bennett, fought till they were surrounded, and then cut their way out through the enemy, losing eight men. The village was then plundered and burned, the savages adding all the atrocities characteristic of their mode of warfare.

Riall next marched his troops through the villages of Youngstown, Tuscarora, and Manchester (now Niagara Falls), and plundered and burned them all, while the terror-stricken inhabitants were butchered or driven away. •Nor was the devastation confined to the villages. For several miles from the river, the houses and barns of the farmers were destroyed, and the women and children either killed or turned shelterless into the woods and fields.

The bridge over Tonawanda Creek had been destroyed by the Americans, and at this point the enemy turned back, and soon recrossed the Niagara to the Canada side.

The alarm at Buffalo brought General Hall, of the New York militia, to that village, where he arrived the day after Christmas. He found collected there a body of seventeen hundred men, whom it would have been gross flattery to call a " force." They were poorly supplied with arms and cartridges, and had no discipline and almost no organization. Another regiment of three hundred soon joined them, but without adding much to their efficiency.

On the 28th of December, Drummond reconnoitred the American camp, and determined to attack it ; for which purpose he sent over General Riall on the evening of the 29th with fourteen hundred and fifty men, largely regulars, and a body of Indians. One detachment landed two miles below Black Rock, crossed Canajokaties Creek in the face of a slight resistance, and took possession of a battery. The remainder landed at a point between Buffalo and Black Rock, under cover of a battery on the Canadian shore. Poor as Hall's troops were, they stood long enough to fire upon the invaders and inflict considerable loss.

As the enemy landed here and formed in battle order, Hall with his raw militia attacked both wings and for a short time made a gallant fight, especially on the American left, where Lieutenant-Colonel Blakeslie handled four hundred Ontario county men remarkably well and disputed the ground with great firmness. Both sides had artillery, with which the action was opened. As it progressed, however, the

American line was broken in the centre, and Hall was compelled to fall back. His subsequent attempts to rally his men were of no avail, and he himself seems to have lost heart ; as Lieutenant Riddle, who had about eighty regulars, offered to place them in front for the encouragement of the militia to new exertion, but Hall declined. Riddle then offered, if Hall would give him two hundred men, to attempt to save the village from destruction, and at least to bring away the women and children, that they might not fall under the tomahawk and scalping-knife ; but even this the General refused, and the village was then left to its fate, though Riddle went in with his own men and rescued the contents of the arsenal and some other property.

Both Buffalo and Black Rock were sacked and burned, and no mercy was shown. With but two or three exceptions, those of the inhabitants who were not able to run away were massacred, many of them being first submitted to torture and indignity. It is related that in Buffalo a widow named St. John " had the address to appease the ferocity of the enemy so far as to remain in her house uninjured." Her house and the stone jail were the only buildings not laid in ashes. In Black Rock every building was either burned or blown up, except one log house, in which a few women and children had taken refuge.

Whether they had the peculiar address necessary to " appease the ferocity of the enemy," or were merely overlooked, is not recorded. Five vessels lying at the wharves were also burned.

In this expedition the British lost a hundred and eight men, killed, wounded, or missing. More than fifty of the Americans were found dead on the field. Truly, an abundant revenge had been taken for the burning of Newark. McClure, who had given the provocation for these atrocities, was an Irishman, and the absurdity of his whole course in the matter seemed calculated to justify the common sarcasms levelled against his countrymen for want of foresight.

All that the Americans had gained on the northern frontier during the year 1813, with the exception of the territory of Michigan, restored by Harrison's victory, had now been lost, and on New Year's day of 1814 the settlers along the whole length of the Niagara—those of them who survived—were shivering beside the smouldering embers of their homes.

CHAPTER X.

WAR IN THE SOUTH.

Engagement at Lewistown—Fight in Delaware Bay—Burning of Havre de Grace, Georgetown, and Fredericktown—Battle at Craney Island—Destruction of Hampton—Troubles with the Southern Indians—Fight at Burnt Corn Creek—Massacre at Fort Mims—Jackson's Campaign—Fights at Talluschatches, Talladega, the Hillabee Towns, Autosse, and Econochaca—Dale's Canoe Fight.

WHILE these costly and almost useless campaigns were being fought at the North, the Southern States were not without their war experiences, which in some instances were quite as bloody. Along the southern Atlantic coast the British had a great advantage from their heavy war-ships, which blockaded the harbors, ran into the navigable inlets, bombarded the towns, and sent parties ashore to plunder and burn. The militia did what they could to repel these incursions, and in some cases, by handling a few pieces of artillery skilfully, drove off the invaders. Lewistown, on Delaware Bay, was bombarded in April. The shells fell short, and the rockets went over the town, but many of the solid shot went through the houses, doing considerable damage. In May, a party of sailors sent ashore to get water for the squadron near Lewistown were spiritedly attacked by militia, and compelled to return to their ships with empty casks. A fortnight later a party was sent ashore for provisions, but was driven off by the vigilant militia before a mouthful had been obtained.

On the 29th of July the British sloop-of-war *Martin* grounded in Delaware Bay, and eight gun-boats and two sloops, commanded by Captain Angus, went down to attack her. They anchored within three quarters of a mile, and opened upon her with all their guns. The frigate *Junon* came to her assistance, and the cannonade was kept up for nearly two hours. The British sailors proved to be very poor gunners, in comparison with the Americans. Hardly a shot struck the gun-boats, while the sloop and the frigate were hulled at almost every discharge. At length the British manned their launches, barges, and cutters, to the number of ten, and pulled off to cut out some of the gun-boats at the end of the line. Eight of them attacked a single gun-boat commanded by Sailing-Master Shead, who used his sweeps to get his craft nearer the squadron, from which it had become separated, but all the while kept firing his twenty-four pounder at his pursuers, striking one or another of them with almost every shot. Finding they were rapidly gaining on him, he anchored and waited for them to attempt boarding. He gave them two more gunfuls, as they drew nigh, with terrible effect, when the piece became disabled. The barges completely surrounded the little gun-boat, and there was a desperate conflict hand-to-hand. But of course it could not last long. Shead's crew were soon overpowered, and the British flag waved triumphantly over his deck. Seven of the British sailors had been killed, and twelve wounded, while seven of Shead's men were wounded.

On the Chesapeake the Americans fared even worse. Early in the morning of the 3d of May, the British Admiral Cockburn sent a force in nineteen barges to destroy the town of Havre de Grace and ravage the country between it and Baltimore. A small battery had been erected for the defence of the place ; but it was still dark when the enemy came, and the first notice the inhabitants had of his approach was given by the balls whistling through the houses. A panic and stampede ensued. But a few men ran to the battery, and fired at the barges till the British began to land, when they all joined in the flight, except an old man named O'Neill, who stood by one of the guns and continued to load and fire it till, in recoiling, it ran over his thigh and somewhat disabled him. He still had strength to get away, armed himself with two muskets, and tried in vain to rally the militia, but finally was taken prisoner. He and his companions at the battery had killed three of the enemy and wounded two.

As soon as the British forces had landed, fire was set to the houses not already destroyed by shells, while the sailors and marines went through them, smashing furniture, cutting open beds to feed the flames, insulting women, and spreading terror. One house only, filled with women, was spared after a special appeal to the Admiral. A church just outside of the town was gutted, farm-houses on the road to Baltimore were plundered, travellers were robbed, and bridges, furnaces, and mills were destroyed.

The little villages of Georgetown and Fredericktown, Maryland, were the next spoil of the Admiral, who led the ravaging party in person. But he did not succeed in landing till his men in the boats had suffered severely from the fire of a battery manned by thirty-five militiamen, which was kept up steadily for half an hour. Not a house was left standing in either of the villages, and the enemy enriched themselves with all the plunder they could carry away.

About this time Admiral Warren, who had issued

from Bermuda a proclamation declaring New York, Charleston, Port Royal, Savannah, and the whole of the Mississippi River under blockade—a paper blockade, at which both Americans and neutrals laughed—joined Admiral Cockburn, in the Chesapeake, and they determined to extend as far as possible the pillaging and burning of towns on the coast.

The next one selected was Norfolk, Va. But the approach to the town was commanded by a battery on Craney Island, and this battery was promptly manned by a hundred American sailors, under command of Lieutenant Neale, of the navy, and fifty marines under Lieutenant Breckenridge. It was dawn of day on the 22d of June when four thousand British sailors and marines, in barges, came in sight of the island; and when they were fairly under the guns of the battery, it blazed out. The pieces were served rapidly and with such precision that many of the barges were cut clear in two, and their occupants would have been drowned had they not been promptly rescued by the others. The Admiral was in a boat fifty feet long, called the *Centipede*, and this was so riddled with shot that he and his crew had barely time to get out of it when it sank. Before this merciless and unremitting fire the squadron of barges at length retreated to the ships. At the same time, a body of eight hundred soldiers had been put ashore, to attack the town by land. But for them a force of Virginia volunteers, under Colonel Beatty, were waiting, with a well-placed battery of six guns. The enemy had not all landed when the battery opened upon them, with such effect that they retreated at once. A part of them took refuge in a house, from which they fired rockets at the battery-men ; but an American gun-boat came up and sent a few twenty-four-pound balls crashing through the house, when the last of the enemy fled, making their way back to the fleet as speedily as possible.

Smarting under this defeat, the British commanders immediately planned the destruction of Hampton, eighteen miles from Norfolk, which they supposed would cut off communication between the latter place and the upper part of Virginia.

At daylight on the 25th, two thousand five hundred soldiers, commanded by Sir Sydney Beckwith, were landed several miles below Hampton, and marched on the town. At the same time, a squadron of boats, commanded by Admiral Cockburn and protected by the sloop-of-war *Mohawk*, drew up before the place and fired in rockets, shells, and solid shot. The entire garrison of the place consisted of six hundred and thirty-six men, commanded by Major Crutchfield, who had seven pieces of artillery.

As Cockburn's barges approached the town, fire was opened upon them with two twelve-pounders, which did so much execution that the Admiral found it discreet to draw off and take position behind a point of land where the American gunners could not see him. From this shelter he fired rockets and shells for an hour, but so wildly that not the slightest damage was effected by them.

Crutchfield sent a company of riflemen, under Captain Servant, with orders to conceal themselves in the woods near the road where Beckwith's column would pass in approaching the town, to annoy and delay it as much as possible. This was done so skilfully as to inflict considerable loss upon the enemy ; and when Crutchfield saw that the barges would not approach the town again till it was in the possession of Beckwith, he marched with the greater part of his force to the assistance of the riflemen, leaving Captain Pryor with a few men to manage the battery and keep off the barges.

Crutchfield's column was fired upon just as the British column had been, by riflemen concealed in a wood ; and as he wheeled to charge upon the hidden foe, he was greeted by a sudden fire from two six-pounders and a discharge of rockets. The

enemy's artillery was so well handled that Crutchfield's column was broken up, and a portion of it
driven from the field.   The remainder made its way
through a defile, all the while under fire, to a junc-
tion with Servant's riflemen.   At the same time Captain Cooper, with what few cavalrymen the Americans had, was annoying the enemy's left flank.

Crutchfield kept up the fighting with spirit as
long as possible, but of course was obliged to give
way at last.   Captain Pryor and his men held their
ground at the battery, preventing any landing from
the barges, till the enemy's land force came up in
the rear and was within sixty yards of the guns.
He then ordered the artillerists to spike the pieces,
and break through the corps of British marines approaching in the rear ; which order was at once
obeyed, to the astonishment of the marines, who
failed to hurt or capture a single man.   With Captain Pryor still at their head, the little band plunged
into a creek and swam across, those who had car-
bines or side-arms taking them with them, and
escaped beyond pursuit.   Crutchfield in his retreat
was followed for two miles by a strong force, which
failed to overtake him, while he frequently halted
his men behind fences and walls, to deliver a volley
at the approaching enemy and then continue the
retreat.

In this fight the British had ninety men killed, and a hundred and twenty wounded. The American loss was seven killed, twelve wounded, and twelve missing.

The village of Hampton was now at the mercy of an enemy who showed no mercy, and was immediately given up to plunder and outrage, which continued for two days and nights. The town was not burned, but every house was ruined as to its furniture and decorations, except the one in which the commanding officers were quartered. Such deeds were perpetrated by the British soldiers and sailors, unrestrained by their officers, as had hardly been paralleled even in Indian warfare. Neither age nor sex nor innocence was any protection. In one case an old and infirm citizen was murdered in the presence of his aged wife ; and when she remonstrated, a soldier presented a pistol at her breast and shot her dead. Women with infants in their arms were pursued till they threw themselves into the river to escape, children were wantonly killed, and such shameful scenes were enacted as cannot even be mentioned in a history written for youth. The soldiers destroyed all the medical stores, that were necessary for the care of the sick and wounded. They also stole a considerable number of slaves and sent them to the West Indies, not to be liberated, but to be sold and turned into cash. When they abandoned the town, they went in such haste that they left behind a large quantity of provisions, arms, and ammunition, and some of their men, who were captured next day by Cooper's cavalry.

The indignation aroused by the unhappy fate of Hampton was such that General Robert R. Taylor, commandant of the district, addressed a letter to Admiral Warren, inquiring whether the outrages were sanctioned by the British commanders, and if not, whether the perpetrators were to be punished. The Admiral referred the letter to Sir Sydney Beckwith, who did not attempt to deny that the outrages had been committed as charged, but said that "the excesses at Hampton, of which General Taylor complains, were occasioned by a proceeding at Craney Island. At the recent attack on that place, the troops in a barge which had been sunk by the fire of the American guns had been fired on by a party of Americans, who waded out and shot these poor fellows while clinging to the wreck of the boat; and with a feeling natural to such a proceeding, the men of that corps landed at Hampton." General Taylor at once appointed a court of inquiry, which by a careful investigation found that none of the men belonging to the wrecked barge had been fired upon, except one who was trying to escape to that division of the British troops which had landed, and he was not killed ; while, so far from shooting the unfortunate men in the water, some of the Americans had waded out to assist them. The report embodying these facts was forwarded to Sir Sydney, who never made any reply — which perhaps is the most nearly graceful thing a man can do when he has been convicted of a deliberate and outrageous falsehood.

In the far South a better success attended the American arms this summer than either on the Northern border or the Atlantic coast. This was owing partly to the greater simplicity of the task that lay before the commanders, and partly to the greater energy with which they entered upon it, but chiefly to the difference in the enemy. In Canada and on the coast, our men contended with forces largely made up of British regulars, at that time perhaps the most efficient soldiery in the world. In Florida and Alabama they contended indeed with British arms, but they were in the hands of Indians.

The English agents at Pensacola, with the connivance of the Spanish authorities there — for Florida belonged to Spain till the United States purchased it in 1819 — had supplied the Creeks with rifles, ammunition, and provisions, and sent them on the war-path, not against the American armies, for there were none in that region, but against the settlers and scattered posts along the navigable rivers. A premium of five dollars was offered for every scalp — whether of man, woman, or child — which the savages might bring to the British agency.

The militia of Georgia, Alabama, and Tennessee were called out to meet the emergency, and before the year was over the Creeks had been made to suffer a terrible retribution.

As one body of these Indians, commanded by a half-breed named McQueen, started for the interior, a militia force under Colonel James Caller set out to intercept them. On the 27th of July they were found encamped on a small, low peninsula enclosed in one of the windings of Burnt Corn Creek. Caller promptly attacked them, and after a sharp action routed them. But he called back the pursuing detachment too soon, the Indians rallied, a part of the whites fled in panic, and the remainder had a severe fight with the savages, in which they were outnumbered and defeated. Caller lost two men killed and fifteen wounded.

This victory inspired the Indians with new confidence, while it spread terror among the settlers. The next hostile movement was against Fort Mims, on Lake Tensas, near Alabama River, forty miles northward of Mobile. This work was a stockade enclosure of about an acre, which a farmer named Mims had erected for the protection of his buildings and cattle. It was loop-holed for musketry all round, and at one corner was an uncompleted block-house. When the alarm of Indian raids had gone forth, the settlers flocked to Fort Mims from all sides, and Governor Claiborne sent a hundred and seventy-five volunteers, under Major Daniel Beasley, to defend it. The space was so crowded that it became necessary to extend the stockade, and another enclosure was made on the eastern side, but the fence between was left standing. On the 29th of August, a thousand Creek warriors, commanded by William Weathersford, a half-breed, arrived within a quarter of a mile of the fort, and concealed themselves in a ravine. Some of them were seen by two Negroes who had been sent out to tend cattle; but when they had given the alarm, and a scouting party had failed to find any trace of Indians, they were not only disbelieved, but severely flogged for lying.

After many false alarms, the occupants of the fort had become incredulous and careless of danger, their commander perhaps most so of all. On the 30th the gates stood wide open, no guard was set,

and when the drum beat for dinner the soldiers laid
aside their arms and went to their meal at the moment when the savages sprang from their hiding-
place and with their well-known yell rushed toward
the stockade. Officers and men sprang to arms at
the frightful sound. Major Beasley, in attempting
to close the outer gate, was knocked down and run
over by the foremost of the assailants, many of
whom poured into the outer enclosure, where they
quickly murdered all the whites whom they found.
Beasley himself crawled off in a corner to die, and
the command devolved upon Captain Bailey.

When the Indians attempted to enter the inner
enclosure, they were stopped by a fire through the
loop-holes in the partition. Five of their prophets,
who had proclaimed that their charms and incanta-
tions rendered the American bullets harmless, all
fell dead at the first discharge. This produced a
temporary check, but new swarms of the naked
savages came up, and a desperate fight through the
loop-holes was maintained for several hours. The
soldiers stood manfully at their posts, were assisted by some of the women and boys, and killed
a large number of the Indians, who, on the other
hand, were sure of hitting somebody whenever they
fired into the crowded enclosure. Numbers of the
red-skins were constantly dancing, hooting, and

yelling around the fort, many of whom were shot by the old men of the garrison, who had ascended to the attic of the largest house and cut holes in the roof.

The enemy were getting tired of this costly work, when Weathersford came up, exhorted them to new efforts, and directed fire-tipped arrows to be shot into the fort. In a short time the buildings were in flames, and the miserable inmates, driven by the heat, were huddled in one corner, when the Indians burst in and rapidly completed the massacre. Children were taken by the heels, and their brains dashed out against the walls; women were butchered in a manner unknown since the wars of the ancient Jews; a few Negroes were kept for slaves, but not one white person was left alive—excepting twelve, who had secretly cut an opening through the stockade and escaped by way of the lake. Of the five hundred and fifty-three persons in the fort at noon, at least four hundred perished before night; and it was believed that about as many of the Indians had been killed or wounded.

The tidings of this massacre of course excited horror and indignation in every part of the country, but nowhere met so prompt and practical a response as in Tennessee. The Legislature of that

State called for thirty-five hundred volunteers — in addition to fifteen hundred whom she had already enrolled in the service of the general Government — voted an appropriation of three hundred thousand dollars, and placed them under command of General Andrew Jackson.*   To General John Cocke was entrusted the work of gathering the troops from East Tennessee, and providing subsistence for the whole. Fayetteville was appointed as the general rendezvous, and Colonel John Coffee was sent forward to Huntsville, Alabama, with a cavalry force of five hundred men, which by the time he arrived there was increased to thirteen hundred.

Jackson reached Fayetteville on the 7th of October, began drilling his men, and on the 11th, hearing from Coffee that the enemy was in sight, marched them to Huntsville — thirty-two miles — in five hours.   For the work in hand, he could not have asked for better material than these Western pioneers, who were skilled in wood-craft, who knew the tricks and manners of the enemy, and were as fearless as they were cunning.   Among them were Sam Houston and the eccentric and now famous David Crockett.

The only serious trouble was in forwarding the

---

* At this time the General was lying helpless at Nashville, from wounds received in a disgraceful affray.

supplies.　At the most southerly point on Tennessee River, while he sent out the cavalry to forage, Jackson drilled the infantry and built Fort Deposit, intended as a depot for provisions when the rise of water should allow them to be sent down.

.Forty-five miles southward, at the Ten Islands of the Coosa, friendly Indians were calling for help against the hostile Creeks.　By a week's march, in which he foraged on all sides and burned several villages, Jackson reached that place.　The enemy were in camp at Talluschatches (now Jacksonville), thirteen miles eastward, and on the night of November 2d Colonel Coffee was sent out with a thousand mounted men and a few friendly Creeks, to attack them.　At sunrise he divided his force into two columns, the heads of which united near the place, while the remainder, swinging outward and forward, made a semicircle about the little town. Within this, two companies were pushed forward to entice the Indians from their shelter.　This accomplished, these companies retreated, and the whole line opened fire upon the savages and rapidly closed in upon them.　"Our men rushed up to the doors of the houses," said Coffee in his report, "and in a few minutes killed the last warrior of them.　The enemy fought with savage fury, and met death with all its horrors, without shrinking or complaining. Not one asked to be spared, but fought as long as they could stand or sit." About two hundred Indians were killed, and eighty-four women and children were made prisoners. The Americans lost five men killed and forty-one wounded.

At this point Jackson was joined after a time by the forces from East Tennessee under General Cocke, and here he built Fort Strother. But before Cocke's arrival he learned that a few friendly Indians in Fort Talladega, thirty miles south, were completely surrounded by a thousand Creeks, who would soon reduce them by starvation. The news was brought by a chief who had disguised himself in a hog-skin and escaped from the fort by night.

Jackson at once put himself at the head of two thousand men, and marched to the relief of the little fort. On the 9th of November he arrived within striking distance of the enemy, when he deployed his columns, placing the volunteers on the right, the militia on the left, and the cavalry on the wings. He adopted precisely the same plan of attack that Coffee had used at Talluschatches; but it was not so completely successful, for two companies of the militia temporarily gave way, and a part of the cavalry had to dismount and fill the gap. Jackson believed that but for this he should have killed every one of the thousand hostile Indians before him. As it was, two hundred and ninety-nine of them were left dead on the field, while the remainder were chased to the mountains, and left a bloody track as they ran. The loss of the whites was fifteen killed and eighty-six wounded.

The Indians of the Hillabee towns, in what is now Cherokee county, sent a messenger to Jackson to sue for peace, through whom he replied that they could only have it on condition of returning prisoners and property and surrendering for punishment those who had been engaged in the massacres. But while they awaited an answer, General Cocke, working his way down the Coosa, sent a force, under General White, to attack these towns. White marched rapidly, destroying everything in his path, and on the 18th of November appeared before the principal village, which he at once fell upon, and killed sixty unresisting Indians, and carried back with him the squaws and children. The Indians, who supposed all the whites were under Jackson's command, looked upon this as a piece of treachery, and became more desperate than ever. For this unfortunate affair, General Cocke has been severely blamed ; but he was tried by a court-martial, and honorably acquitted, while his own published statement makes it clear that he acted in entire good faith.   He was as destitute of provisions as Jackson was, and thought if he pushed on to Fort Strother it would only double the number of starving soldiers there.

While Jackson was coming down from the north, General John Floyd, with nine hundred and fifty Georgians and four hundred Indians, was coming from the east.   He first found the enemy at Autosse, on the Tallapoosa, thirty miles east of the present site of Montgomery, where, on the 29th of November, he attacked them, drove them from their villages to holes and caves in the river-bank, burned all their dwellings, and then hunted down and killed as many of them as possible.   At least two hundred fell.   The whites lost eleven killed and fifty-four wounded.

General Ferdinand L. Claiborne entered the country from the west in July, and built small forts at various points.   On the 12th of December he left Fort Claiborne (on the site of the present town of that name) with a thousand men, and after marching more than a hundred miles northeast, he came on the 23d to an Indian town of refuge, called Econochaca, on the Alabama, west of Montgomery. This village was built upon what the Indian prophets assured the tribe was holy ground, which no white man could set foot upon and live.   No path of any kind led to it.　Here the women and children had been sent for safety; here, in a little square, the prophets performed their religious rites, which are supposed to have included the burning of captives at the stake.　Several captives, of both sexes, it is said were standing with the wood piled about them when Claiborne's columns appeared before the town.

The Indians, who had hurried their women and children across the river, fought desperately for a short time, and then broke and fled, many of them swimming the river and escaping.　About thirty were killed.　The whites lost one killed and six wounded.　Claiborne sacked and burned the village, and then returned to Fort Claiborne, where his forces rapidly melted away by the expiration of their terms of service.　Jackson, at Fort Strother, was in a similar predicament; and thus closed the year on the campaign at the South.　It had been attended with many instances of individual bravery and exciting and romantic adventure, one of the most famous of which is known as the Canoe Fight, of which General Samuel Dale was the hero.　There can be no better account of it than Dale's own, as he related it some years afterward to his friend Hon. John H. F. Claiborne, who incorporated it in his " Life of Dale."　The General was on his way,

November 13th, with sixty men, to attack an Indian camp on the east side of the Alabama, near what is now Dale's Ferry.   He says :

"I put thirty of my men on the east bank, where the path ran directly by the river-side.   With twenty men I kept the western bank, and thus we proceeded to Randon's Landing.   A dozen fires were burning, and numerous scaffolds for drying meat, denoting a large body of Indians ; but none were visible.   About half past ten A.M. we discerned a large canoe coming down stream.   It contained eleven warriors.   Observing that they were about to land at a cane-brake just above us, I called to my men to follow, and dashed for the cane-brake with all my might.   Only seven of my men kept up with me.   As the Indians were in the act of landing, we fired.   Two leaped into the water. Jim Smith shot one as he rose, and I shot the other. In the mean time they had backed into deep water, and three Indians were swimming on the off side of the canoe, working her as far from the shore as they could, to get out of the range of our guns. The others lay in the bottom of the canoe, which was thirty odd feet long, four feet deep, and three feet beam, made of an immense cypress-tree, specially for the transportation of corn.   One of the warriors shouted to Weathersford (who was in the vicinity, as it afterward appeared, but invisible to us), '*Yos-ta-hah! yos-ta-hah!*' 'They are spoiling us.' This fellow was in the water, his hands on the gunwale of the pirogue, and as often as he rose to shout we fired, but ineffectually. He suddenly showed himself breast-high, whooping in derision, and said, 'Why don't you shoot?' I drew my sight just between his hands, and as he rose I lodged a bullet in his brains. Their canoe then floated down with the current. I ordered my men on the east bank to fetch the boats. Six of them jumped into a canoe, and paddled to the Indians, when one of them cried out, 'Live Indians! Back water, boys! back water!' and the frightened fellows paddled back whence they came. I next ordered Cæsar, a free Negro fellow, to bring a boat. Seeing him hesitate, I swore I would shoot him the moment I got across. He crossed a hundred yards below the Indians, and Jim Smith, Jerry Austill, and myself got in. I made Cæsar paddle within forty paces, when all three of us levelled our guns, and all missed fire! As the two boats approached, one of them hurled his scalping-knife at me. It pierced the boat through and through, just grazing my thigh as it passed. The next moment the canoes came in contact. I leaped up, placing one of my feet in each boat. At the same instant the foremost warrior levelled his rifle at my breast. It flashed in the pan. As quick as lightning, he clubbed it, and aimed at me a furious blow, which I partially parried, and, before he could repeat it, I shivered his skull with my gun. In the mean time an Indian had struck down Jerry, and was about to despatch him, when I broke my rifle over his head. It parted in two places. The barrel Jerry seized, and renewed the fight. The stock I hurled at one of the savages. Being then disarmed, Cæsar handed me his musket and bayonet.

"Finding myself unable to keep the two canoes in juxtaposition, I resolved to bring matters to an issue, and leaped into the Indian boat. My pirogue, with Jerry, Jim, and Cæsar, floated off. Jim fired, and slightly wounded the Indian next to me. I now stood in the centre of their canoe — two dead at my feet — a wounded savage in the stern, who had been snapping his piece at me during the fight, and four powerful warriors in front. The first one directed a furious blow at me with his rifle ; it glanced upon the barrel of my musket, and I staved the bayonet through his body. As he fell, the next one repeated the attack. A shot from Jerry Austill pierced his heart. Striding over them, the next sprung at me with his tomahawk. I killed him with the bayonet, and his corpse lay between me and the last of the party. I knew him well — Tar-cha-chee, a noted wrestler, and the most famous ball-player of his clan. He paused a moment in expectation of my attack, but, finding me motionless, he stepped backward to the bow of the canoe, shook himself, gave the war-whoop of his tribe, and cried out, 'Sam tholocco *Iana dahmaska, ia-lanestha — lipso — lipso — lanestha. Big Sam! I am a man — I am coming — come on!*' As he said this, with a terrific yell he bounded over the dead body of his comrade, and directed a blow at my head with his rifle, which dislocated my left shoulder. I dashed the bayonet into him. It glanced round his ribs, and the point hitching to his back-bone, I pressed him down. As I pulled the weapon out, he put his hands upon the sides of the canoe and endeavored to rise, crying out, '*Tar-cha-chee is a man. He is not afraid to die!*' I drove my bayonet through his heart. I then turned to the wounded villain in the stern, who snapped his rifle at me as I advanced, and had been snapping during the whole conflict. He gave the war-whoop, and, in tones of hatred and defiance, exclaimed, '*I am a warrior — I am not afraid to die.*' As he uttered the words I pinned him down with my bayonet, and he followed his eleven comrades to the land of spirits.

" During this conflict, which was over in ten minutes, my brave companions, Smith and Austill, had been struggling with the current of the Alabama, endeavoring to reach me. Their guns had become useless, and their only paddle had been broken. Two braver fellows never lived. Austill's first shot saved my life.

" By this time my men came running down the bank, shouting that Weathersford was coming. With our three canoes we crossed them all over, and got safely back to the fort."

CHAPTER XI.

NAVAL BATTLES OF 1813.

The Hornet and the Peacock—The Chesapeake and the Shannon—The Argus and the Pelican—The Enterprise and the Boxer—Decatur blockaded at New London—A New Embargo.

THE brilliant victories achieved on the ocean in 1812 reversed the opinion the Government had entertained as to the value of the navy, and early in 1813 Congress authorized the building of four ships-of-the-line, six frigates, six sloops-of-war, and as many vessels on the lakes as the service might require.

But in the second year of the war the American sailor did not meet with that uniform success which in the first year had surprised and confounded the self-styled Mistress of the Seas. One battle, in which a noble ship was lost and many lives were sacrificed, through drunkenness, was a grievous mortification to the whole American people. The commander of the defeated vessel was fortunate in not surviving the action, as he would probably have been court-martialled and disgraced.

The first naval engagement of the year took place in West Indian waters. Lieutenant James Law-

rence, in the *Hornet*, of twenty guns, was cruising up and down the coast of Guiana, and had taken a few prizes, when on the 24th of February he sighted the English brig *Peacock*, Captain Peake, which also carried twenty guns. Both vessels were cleared for action, and at five o'clock in the afternoon bore down upon each other. They passed within half pistol-shot ; and as they passed, each delivered the full broadside of the larboard battery. The *Peacock* then put her helm hard up, intending to wear round and rake the *Hornet*. But Lawrence quickly imitated the movement, got the better of his antagonist, and with all his guns blazing bore down upon her quarter. He then closed, and kept up so terrific a fire that in fifteen minutes from the beginning of the action the Englishman not only struck his colors, but hoisted them in the fore-rigging with the union down — which is a signal of distress. A few minutes later, the *Peacock's* main-mast tumbled.

An officer sent on board to take possession found that she had six feet of water in the hold, and was settling rapidly. Captain Peake and four of his men had been killed, and thirty-three wounded. Every effort was made to save the wounded men. Both vessels anchored, for the water here was but thirty-three feet deep. The prisoners were removed as fast as possible, while, to keep the *Peacock* afloat, her guns were thrown overboard, the shot-holes plugged, and the pumps manned ; but in spite of all exertions she went down, carrying nine of her own crew and three of the *Hornet's.* Four of the prisoners lowered the stern boat, which was supposed to be so damaged as to be useless, and paddled ashore in it. Four others climbed into the rigging of the fore-top, and as this remained above the surface when the hull touched bottom, they were saved. On the *Hornet* one man had been killed and two wounded by the enemy's fire, and her rigging was considerably damaged.

As another British war-vessel was not far away, the *Hornet* had to be put in fighting trim again with all speed, which was accomplished within four hours after the action. As she was crowded with prisoners and was short of water, she turned her prow toward home, arriving at Martha's Vineyard on the the 19th of March, and proceeding through Long Island Sound to New York. Congress voted Lawrence a gold medal, and to each of his commissioned officers a silver one ; and he was soon promoted to the rank of captain, and given command of the frigate *Chesapeake,* then lying in Boston harbor. The very next naval battle was the one in which Lawrence lost his life, lost his ship, and lost a great part of his reputation.

Captain Philip Bowes Vere Broke, commanding the British frigate *Shannon*, of thirty-eight guns, had been cruising along the New England coast for some time, looking for prizes, and especially for an opportunity to retrieve the honor of his flag in an encounter with some American war-ship of the size of his own. Lawrence was preparing for a cruise against the English fleet engaged in the Greenland whale-fishery; but when the *Shannon* appeared in the offing, June 1st, he hastily got his crew together and went out from Boston to fight her.

Broke had sent in to him a letter containing a formal challenge to try the powers of the two ships; but it did not arrive till the *Chesapeake* had sailed, and Lawrence never received it. One sentence of this letter is very significant, in that it contains the whole germ of the war. "I doubt not that you, equally confident of success, will feel convinced that it is only by repeated triumphs in even combats that your little navy can now hope to console your country for the loss of that trade it can no longer protect." That was it exactly. American trade, the grudge of British merchants, and the constant object of British hostilities, was to be permitted only so far as American guns were able to protect it; and since the American navy, as Captain Broke said, was little, while England's was large, it was confidently believed by his countrymen that this protection would not ultimately amount to much.

At six o'clock in the evening the vessels came within cannon-shot of each other, and the *Shannon* opened fire at once. But the *Chesapeake* remained silent till her whole broadside could be brought to bear; then she opened her ports, and for eight minutes there was a terrific and continuous roar. Now, as before, the Americans were the better gunners, and in this broadside firing the advantage was with the *Chesapeake;* but accident favored her antagonist and gave him an opportunity to use the advantages he possessed in other respects. Two or three shots that struck the rigging of the *Chesapeake* rendered her for a short time not perfectly manageable, and her mizzen-rigging fouled in the *Shannon's* fore-chains. This exposed her to a raking fire, and her upper deck was swept at once by two of the enemy's guns.

In the broadside firing, Captain Lawrence had been wounded in the leg, the master was killed, the first lieutenant was disabled, and the marine officer, the fourth lieutenant, and the boatswain were mortally wounded. So great a proportion of officers struck down was a rare accident. To increase the misfortune, a Negro bugler had been substituted for the drummer, and when Lawrence ordered the signal to be sounded for boarding, it was found that the bugleman had crawled under the launch, and when he was hauled out he was still so frightened that he could not sound a note. Lawrence then passed down verbal orders for the boarders to come on deck, and at this moment he fell, shot through the body. As he was carried below, he exclaimed : "Tell the men to fire faster, and not give up the ship. Fight her till she sinks!"

But it was too late. The enemy were already on his deck in great numbers, and after a short and unorganized resistance his men were overcome and his ship was captured. The victors considerably increased the casualties by firing down the hatchways with musketry, in justification of which it is said that some one had fired up the hatch and killed a marine.

The havoc in both crews had been frightful for so short a battle. On the *Shannon*, twenty-four were killed and fifty-eight wounded ; on the *Chesapeake* forty-seven were killed and ninety-eight wounded. Nearly one third of all the men engaged in the action had been struck. Captain Lawrence died in four days. His age was but thirty-one. He had been greatly admired for his personal bravery, his courteousness, his regard for the sailors under his command, and his wonderful nautical skill.

In explanation of this defeat, it is said that Captain Broke had been for weeks giving his men a special training for such an encounter; while the *Chesapeake* had a heterogeneous crew, a part of them were new men, and many of the old ones were in a state of half mutiny from not having received prize money that was due them. Some of the officers were sick on shore, others were inexperienced, and several of the sailors were seen drunk in the streets of Boston an hour before they were summoned to go on board as the vessel was weighing anchor. These facts seem to be well established; but the explanation does not make it any the less a British victory. If Broke's men were under good discipline, while Lawrence's were not, he is entitled to as much credit for his achievement as if it had been accomplished through superior courage or any other means. And Lawrence, had he not died, might properly have been censured, or even punished, for going out to fight under such circumstances, when he could have waited till he had trained his crew. It was also said that the sailors entertained a superstitious belief that the *Chesapeake* was an unlucky ship. It was she that had been fired into by the *Leopard*, in 1807, when she had not a single gun in condition to return the shot; and just before her battle with the

Shannon she had cruised across the Atlantic to the coast of Africa, and home again by way of the West Indies, without taking a single prize.

Broke's victory was a grateful salve to England's pride, so sorely wounded by the naval events of 1812, and her historians have never tired of dwelling upon it. One of the latest of them devotes more than eight pages to it alone, while he disposes of all the other sea-fights of this war in less than three.

The American brig *Argus*, of twenty guns, commanded by Captain William Henry Allen, after taking Hon. William H. Crawford to France as the new United States Minister at the French court, made a cruise in the English and Irish channels, where she captured twenty merchantmen. But in the evening of August 13th she had the misfortune to capture a vessel loaded with wine. The crew spent most of the night in transferring the cargo, and helped themselves liberally to the contents of some of the casks. Just before daylight, when all of them were tired out and many were intoxicated, they completed their misfortune by setting fire to the prize.

By the light of the burning vessel, the British brig *Pelican*, of twenty-one guns, sighted the *Argus* and bore down upon her. The *Pelican* got the weather-gage, and came within close range. The *Argus* opened with a broadside, and for three quarters of an hour the firing was kept up on both sides with great spirit. At the end of that time the American had lost her steering apparatus and most of her running rigging, while the enemy was lying under her stern, firing at leisure. Captain Allen was mortally wounded before the fighting had been going on five minutes, and his first lieutenant was disabled a few minutes later. There was now nothing for the *Argus* but to surrender. She had lost six men killed and seventeen wounded ; the *Pelican*, three killed and five wounded.

Early in September the American brig *Enterprise*, of fourteen guns, commanded by Lieutenant William Burrows, was cruising along the coast of Maine in search of Canadian privateers, when, on the 5th, near Penguin Point, within sight of Portland, the British brig *Boxer*, of fourteen guns, Captain Samuel Blythe, was encountered. Both vessels prepared for action, and a few minutes past three o'clock they had approached within half pistol-shot, when both opened fire. The wind was light, the sea nearly smooth, and the broadsides of the *Enterprise* were very effective. Burrows had mounted a long gun in his poop-cabin, running it out of a window, and after the first broadside he drew ahead, sheered across the enemy's bow, and raked him with this gun. This was repeated, with other skilful manœuvres, and in forty minutes the *Boxer*, being hailed, said she was ready to surrender, but could not haul down her colors, because they were nailed to the mast.

One of her officers is said to have sprung upon a gun, shaken his fists at the Americans, in a fearful state of excitement, and shouted "No! no! no!" adding a few opprobrious epithets, when a superior officer ordered him down. This exhibition, together with the ridiculous fact that a ship with her colors nailed was trying to surrender, brought a hearty laugh from the American crew, notwithstanding the shattered spars and bloody decks.

The *Enterprise* immediately ceased firing, and took possession of the prize. The American vessel had suffered very little injury, though her hull was peppered with grapeshot, a ball had passed through her foremast and one through her mainmast, and her upper rigging was considerably cut. She had lost one man killed and thirteen wounded, three of them mortally. The *Boxer* had been hulled repeatedly, three balls had passed through her foremast, some of her guns were dismounted, her top-gallant forecastle was cut away, and her rigging badly injured. The number of her men that were killed has never been ascertained ; fourteen were wounded. The commanders of the two vessels both fell, almost at the same moment : Blythe cut in two by an eighteen-pound ball, Burrows mortally wounded by a canister-shot. They were buried side by side in Portland, with the honors of war.

The poet Longfellow, who at that time was in his seventh year and lived in Portland, alludes to this battle in his poem entitled " My Lost Youth."

> " I remember the sea-fight far away,
>   How it thundered o'er the tide !
> And the dead captains, as they lay
> In their graves, o'erlooking the tranquil bay
>   Where they in battle died.
>   And the sound of that mournful song
>   Goes through me with a thrill :
>   ' A boy's will is the wind's will,
> And the thoughts of youth are long, long thoughts.' "

On the day when the *Chesapeake* was captured by the *Shannon*, three American war-vessels, under Commodore Decatur — the *United States*, the *Macedonian*, and the *Hornet* — were driven into the harbor of New London, Conn., by a superior force of British ships, and so rigorously was the blockade of the port kept up, that not one of the three got to sea again during the war. At the same time the land defences, manned by Connecticut militia, prevented the blockading squadron from entering the harbor to attack them. Decatur made many attempts to get out with his fleet, but was always frustrated by the vigilance of the blockaders, which he believed was assisted by traitors on shore. He declared that whenever he planned an escape, the enemy were warned of his intention by blue lights burned at the mouth of the harbor ; and from this circumstance the opprobrious name of "Blue-Lights" was applied to the Federal party, which had opposed the war. It is not unlikely that something of this sort was done, either by traitors or by spies in the employ of the blockaders ; but that the Federal party of Connecticut had anything to do with it is sufficiently refuted by the fact that the Connecticut militia, largely Federalists, not only protected Decatur's vessels when they might have permitted them to be captured, but rendered some distinguished services before the war was over, especially in the gallant defence of Stonington. Still the Federalists continued to oppose the war, though in a hopeless minority as to the whole country, and, like all parties out of power, sharply and unceasingly criticised the Administration. Their criticisms, too, were sometimes based on pretty strong facts, as, for instance, when they ridiculed the idea that it was a war for sailors' rights, by quoting an official circular to collectors of customs which forbade them to grant protections to Negro sailors. Even thus early were some of our politicians imbued with the notion that the color of a man's skin must necessarily make a vast difference with his rights under the government for which he paid taxes and bore arms.

The freedom of the Massachusetts coast from blockade was a source of irritation to the more southerly States ; and when in December, 1813, the President complained to Congress that supplies were furnished to British cruisers, and other contraband trade was carried on through the ports of the Bay State, Congress laid a new embargo on the exportation, either by land or water, of any goods, produce, live stock, or specie. A similar embargo bill had passed the House of Representatives in July, but was then defeated in the Senate.

Up to the close of 1813, the English had captured from the Americans seven vessels of war, mounting one hundred and nineteen guns. In the same time, the Americans had captured from the English twenty-six vessels of war, mounting five hundred and sixty guns.

CHAPTER XII.

PRIVATEERS.

IN the naval operations of this, as of the preceding year, privateers played an important part. A large number had been commissioned ; during the entire war, the whole number set afloat was two hundred and fifty-one. Fifty-eight of these belonged in the port of Baltimore, fifty-five in New York, forty in Salem, Mass., thirty-one in Boston, fourteen in Philadelphia, eleven in Portsmouth, N. H., and ten in Charleston, S. C.

These vessels were commonly small, or of moderate size, and were swift sailers. They carried a few broadside guns ; but the peculiar feature of their armament was a long gun, generally an eighteen-pounder, mounted on the deck and turning on a swivel, so that it could be instantly pointed in any direction, no matter what might be the position of the vessel. This gun was called Long Tom.

These privateers not only captured merchant

ships, but even fought with the smaller naval vessels of the enemy, and sometimes conquered them. And they often had a double character, taking cargoes of merchandise for distant ports and at the same time-being ready to fight on the way.

There was in 1812, as there has been since, more or less sentimental objection to privateering, which had come down from the days when privateers and pirates were the same. The argument in favor of the system was set forth with great clearness by Thomas Jefferson, in an article published about a month after the war began. He said :

"What is war? It is simply a contest between nations of trying which can do the other the most harm. Who carries on the war? Armies are formed and navies manned by individuals. How is a battle gained? By the death of individuals. What produces peace? The distress of individuals. What difference to the sufferer is it that his property is taken by a national or private armed vessel? Did our merchants, who have lost nine hundred and seventeen vessels by British captures, feel any gratification that the most of them were taken by his Majesty's men-of-war? Were the spoils less rigidly exacted by a seventy-four-gun ship than by a privateer of four guns? and were not all equally condemned? War, whether on land or sea, is constituted of acts of violence on the persons and property of individuals ; and excess of violence is the grand cause that brings about a peace. One man fights for wages paid him by the Government, or a patriotic zeal for the defence of his country ; another, duly authorized, and giving the proper pledges for good conduct, undertakes to pay himself at the expense of the foe, and serve his country as effectually as the former, and Government, drawing all its supplies from the people, is in reality as much affected by the losses of the one as the other, the efficacy of its measures depending upon the energies and resources of the whole.

"In the United States, every possible encouragement should be given to privateering in time of war with a commercial nation. We have tens of thousands of seamen that without it would be destitute of the means of support, and useless to their country. Our national ships are too few to give employment to a twentieth part of them, or retaliate the acts of the enemy. But by licensing private armed vessels, the whole naval force of the nation is truly brought to bear on the foe ; and while the contest lasts, that it may have the speedier termination, let every individual contribute his mite, in the best way he can, to distress and harass the enemy and compel him to peace."

The truth is, privateering is the most merciful part of war ; for it damages the enemy by capturing property rather than by destroying life, and in so doing it throws the immediate burden upon the commercial community behind the armies, who have to a large extent the power of making war and peace without personal risk to themselves, and often exhibit a willingness to sacrifice the lives of soldiers with the greatest freedom, so long as their own property is secure. Show them that their property is not secure in war, and you give them a strong motive for making peace. In modern times, the men who are to risk their lives if war arises, generally have little to say on the question whether there shall be a war ; while those who are to risk their ships and cargoes, often have a determining voice. The greater that risk, the less the probability of war.

When the great powers of Europe drew up and signed the Treaty of Paris in 1856, they abolished privateering, so far as they were concerned. The lesser powers of Europe, and some of those on this continent, accepted the general invitation to join in the treaty. The United States Government replied that it would join in it, provided a clause were inserted to the effect that private property on the high seas, if not contraband of war, should be exempt from seizure not only by privateers but by the public armed vessels of an enemy. The great powers that originally made the treaty refused to insert any such clause; thereby confessing that their object was not to exempt private property from the burdens and derangements of war, but merely to control the mode of its seizure, and to secure for themselves with their large navies an advantage over nations that in time of peace have small navies or none at all. So the United States retains to this day her right to send out privateers if she becomes involved in war with any maritime people.

One at least of the London journals, the *Statesman*, foresaw the danger from privateers in 1812. When war was threatened, it said : "America cannot certainly pretend to wage a maritime war with us. She has no navy to do it with. But America has nearly a hundred thousand as good seamen as any in the world, all of whom would be actively employed against our trade on every part of the ocean, in their fast-sailing ships of war, many of which will be able to cope with our small cruisers ; and they will be found to be sweeping the West India seas, and even carrying desolation into the chops of the Channel."

All this, and more, the two hundred and fifty privateers accomplished. They cruised in every sea, and wrought such havoc with British commerce as had never been known before. Coggeshall's history of the service enumerates about fifteen hundred prizes taken by them in the two and a half years of war, and these were not all of the captures by privateers alone ; while the government war-vessels, in their cruises, added considerably to the number.

The fortunes of the privateers were of the most varied kind. Some of them made long cruises without falling in with a single British merchantman of which they could make a prize. Others took enough to enrich every man of the crew. The *Surprise*, of Baltimore, took twenty in a single month. The *True-Blooded Yankee* was one of the most daring and most fortunate. On one cruise she took twenty-seven prizes in thirty-seven days. On the same cruise she captured a small island on the coast of Ireland, and held possession of it for six days. She also took a small seaport town of Scotland, and burned seven vessels in the harbor. A partial list of the spoils with which she was laden when she arrived in a French port, will give some idea of the business. She had eighteen bales of Turkish carpets, forty-three bales of raw silk, weighing six tons, twenty boxes of gums, twenty-four packs of beaver skins, one hundred and sixty dozen swan skins, forty-six packs of other skins, a hundred and ninety hides, a quantity of copper, and various other articles.

The *York*, of Baltimore, after cruising on the coast of Brazil and through the West Indies, returned home with prizes valued at $1,500,000.

The *Snapdragon*, of Newbern, N. C., captured a brig with a cargo, mainly dry goods, worth half a million dollars, and got safely into port with her.

The *Saucy Jack*, of Charleston, took the ship *Mentor*, with a cargo valued at $300,000, and sent her into New Orleans ; and a short time afterward the same privateer took a brig with $60,000 worth of dry goods.

The *Yankee*, in a cruise of a hundred and fifty days, scoured the whole western coast of Africa, taking eight prizes, and came home with thirty-two bales of fine goods, six tons of ivory, and $40,000 in gold dust ; all together worth nearly $300,000.

The *Leo*, of Baltimore, captured an East Indiaman worth two and a half million dollars, which was recaptured by an English sloop-of-war, though not till the *Leo* had taken off $60,000 in bullion.

The *Governor Tompkins*, of New York, near the Madeira Islands captured the *Nereid*, with an assorted cargo valued at $375,000.

The *St. Lawrence*, with a cargo valued at over $300,000, was captured and sent into Portsmouth,

N. H., where she was proved to be an English vessel, and condemned, though she had professed to be American.

Perhaps the most valuable single prize taken in the war was the *Queen*, captured by the *General Armstrong*, of New York. She carried sixteen guns, and was not taken without a stubborn fight, in which her captain, first lieutenant, and nine men were killed. She was valued at nearly $500,000, but on her way into port was wrecked off Nantucket.

One prize contained wine and raisins valued at $75,000 ; another, $70,000 worth of cotton ; another, $20,000 worth of indigo ; another, seven hundred tons of mahogany ; another $70,000 worth of rum and sugar ; another, $150,000 worth of gums, almonds, and beeswax ; another, $23,000 in specie, and still another, $80,000 in specie.

All this looks very much like robbery, and in truth it was robbery, unless the war, on the part of the Americans, was justifiable. But it is certainly more humane to conquer the enemy by robbing his merchants than by killing his men ; and there can be no question that the exploits of these privateers did more to bring the war between England and the United States to an end, and prevent another one, than drawn battles, however gallantly fought, and futile expeditions against Canada.

But the exploits of the privateers did not consist solely in plundering unarmed merchantmen. They were often pursued and attacked by British men-of-war, and some of the English packet-ships carried heavy guns, and would not surrender without a desperate fight.

The privateer schooner *Governor Tompkins*, a few days after the capture of the *Nereid* in December, 1812, gave chase to what appeared to be a large merchantman. But she proved to be a frigate in disguise, and a sudden squall sent the schooner under her guns before she could change her course. The frigate opened fire at once, and her first broadside killed two men and wounded six. It also blew up a box of cartridges and set fire to some pistols and tube-boxes in the companion-way, all of which exploded and went flying in every direction. The schooner's little battery returned the fire, but her principal exertions were to get out of the way of her powerful antagonist. A chase of two hours ensued, during most of which time the vessels were within gunshot and the firing was kept up. The *Tompkins* threw overboard all the lumber from the deck, and two thousand pounds of shot, and got out her sweeps, and so escaped. Her captain, Nathaniel Shaler, said in a letter describing the action : "The name of one of my poor fellows who

was killed ought to be registered on the book of
fame, and remembered with reverence as long as
bravery is considered a virtue.   He was a black
man, by the name of John Johnson.   A twenty-four-
pound shot struck him in the hip, and took away
all the lower part of his body.   In this state the
poor, brave fellow lay on the deck and several times
exclaimed to his shipmates, 'Fire away, boys!
neber haul de color down!'   The other was also a
black man, by the name of John Davis, and was
struck in much the same way.   He fell near me,
and several times requested to be thrown overboard,
saying he was only in the way of the others."

Captain Boyle, in the privateer *Comet*, of Baltimore, made a remarkable cruise, early in 1813, on
the coast of Brazil and in the West Indies.   On the
14th of January he overhauled a Portuguese brig-of-
war which was convoying three English merchantmen — a ship and two brigs — from Pernambuco.
Boyle informed the captain that he had no right to
do anything of the sort, and that he should proceed to make prizes of them.   As the man-of-war
insisted on protecting them, there was a fight — one
vessel against four, for the merchantmen were
heavily armed.   It began at half past eight o'clock
in the evening, and was carried on by moonlight.
Every vessel had on a crowd of canvas.   The *Comet*

ran alongside the ship and one of the brigs, and opened her broadside upon both of them. The man-of-war then fired grape and round shot into the *Comet*, which returned the compliment, but stuck close to the merchantmen. They frequently separated, to give the man-of-war a chance at the privateer, when the privateer would pour a whole broadside into them, and then turn his attention to the larger antagonist. An hour after midnight, the ship, which had been badly cut to pieces and rendered unmanageable, struck her flag; and soon afterward the two brigs, which had been almost as badly damaged, surrendered. All this while the man-of-war was hovering near and exchanging occasional broadsides with the *Comet*, till the moon set, and it became dark and squally. One of the brigs had been taken possession of by Boyle ; the other and the ship, assisted by the man-of-war, escaped him and made their way back to Pernambuco. On the man-of-war the first lieutenant and five men were killed, and several wounded, the captain mortally.

On the 25th of the same month, the privateer *Dolphin*, Captain W. S. Stafford, cruising off the coasts of Spain and Portugal, fell in with a large ship and a brig, and fought them both. The privateer carried ten guns, the ship sixteen, and the brig ten.   After a spirited action, in which the *Dolphin* lost four men, she captured both of them, and sent them home to Baltimore. The same privateer, in November, was attacked just outside of Charleston harbor by five boats from an English man-of-war. Captain Stafford tore one of the boats to pieces by a discharge of grape-shot, and as the other boats had employment enough in saving their unfortunate comrades, the attack failed. The man-of-war then fired a broadside at the *Dolphin* and sailed away.

The privateer *Lottery*, Captain Southcomb, while at anchor in Chesapeake Bay, February 15th, was captured by nine British barges, in which were two hundred and forty men ; but not till after a fight of an hour and a half, in which the six guns of the *Lottery* had made sickening havoc with the men in the crowded barges. Captain Southcomb was badly wounded.

On the 11th of March the privateer *General Armstrong*, Captain Guy R. Champlin, of New York, encountered, off Surinam, what she supposed to be an English privateer. The *Armstrong* bore down upon her, fired the starboard broadside, wore ship and gave her the larboard broadside, and was then about to attempt boarding, but found out that the enemy was a frigate, carrying twenty-four guns. The battle lasted three quarters of an hour, when the *Arm-strong* succeeded in getting away.   Captain Champlin, badly wounded, lay on the cabin floor, directly over the magazine, with a pistol in his hand, when he overheard some talk about striking the colors. He immediately ordered the surgeon to go on deck and tell the men that if any one of them dared to strike the colors, he would discharge his pistol into the magazine and blow them all up together.   In his log-book he wrote : " In this action we had six men killed and sixteen wounded, and all the halyards of the headsails shot away ; the fore-mast and bowsprit one quarter cut through, and all the fore and main shrouds but one shot away ; both main-stays and running rigging cut to pieces ; a great number of shot through our sails, and several between wind and water, which caused our vessel to leak.   There were also a number of shot in our hull.''

The privateer *Young Teazer* met a singular fate. In June she was chased by a British man-of-war. Her lieutenant had been once captured, and released on parole, and had gone into the service again without waiting to be exchanged.   When he saw a probability of another capture, he seized a firebrand and ran into the cabin, and in another moment the vessel was blown to fragments, and every man on board perished, except seven sailors who were standing on the forecastle.

The privateer *Wasp*, carrying two guns, had a battle of nine hours' duration, on the 31st of July, with the British war-schooner *Bream*, of ten guns. For the last forty-five minutes the action was at close quarters, and the *Wasp* then surrendered.

In August the privateer *Decatur*, carrying seven guns, Captain Dominique Diron, was cruising in the track of West India traders, when on the 5th she encountered the English war-schooner *Dominica*, of sixteen guns, and after a bloody battle captured her. It was at first a running fight, the *Dominica* firing frequent broadsides, and the *Decatur* answering with her Long Tom and volleys of musketry. After several futile attempts to board, Captain Diron succeeded in forcing his bowsprit over the enemy's stern, and sending the jib-boom through her mainsail. The next moment, while a part of his crew kept up the musketry fire, the remainder rushed on board the *Dominica*, and a hand-to-hand slaughter at once began. Men were cut down with swords, and shot with pistols, till the deck was covered with the dead and wounded. The English crew did not surrender till their captain, G. W. Barrette, was killed, all the other officers except the surgeon and one midshipman either killed or wounded, and altogether sixty men disabled. Of the *Decatur's* men, five were killed and fifteen wounded.

The *Globe* privateer had a desperate fight, on the 3d of November, with two heavily armed packet brigs. Broadside after broadside was exchanged at the distance of a few yards, and the brigs were compelled to strike. But when the *Globe* hauled alongside to take possession of one of them, she raised her colors again and fired a broadside ; after which both brigs sailed slowly away, while the *Globe*, which had lost twenty-three men, was too badly crippled to follow.

The privateer *Saratoga*, of four guns, captured the English mail packet *Morgiana*, which carried eighteen guns, by boarding. There was an obstinate defence, and two of the packet's men were killed and five wounded, while the *Saratoga* lost three killed and seven wounded. During the fight the mail was thrown overboard.

Near the Canary Islands a British sloop-of-war decoyed the privateer *Grampus* under her guns, and then suddenly opened her ports and gave her a whole broadside at half pistol-shot. This discharge killed the captain and one man and wounded several others, and damaged the rigging badly, so that the *Grampus* escaped with difficulty.

On Monday, the 5th of July, the *Yankee*, a fishing-smack, was fitted out in New York harbor to capture by stratagem the British sloop-of-war *Eagle*. A calf, a sheep, a goose, and three fishermen were placed conspicuously on the deck, while below were concealed forty men armed with muskets. She then sailed down the bay. The *Eagle* overhauled her, and ordered her to report to the Commodore. Suddenly, at the signal word "Lawrence," the forty men appeared, levelled their muskets across the deck of the *Eagle*, and with one volley killed three of her men and drove the others below. She struck without firing a gun, and as she was taken up the harbor she was greeted by the cheers of a multitude of people who were on the Battery, celebrating Independence day.

While an American fishing-smack was thus capturing a British sloop-of-war in the harbor of New York, on the other side of the ocean the London *Evening Star* was just saying: "The American navy must be annihilated; her arsenals and dock-yards consumed. The American merchant-vessels ought perhaps to be permitted to arm against the pirates of the Mediterranean or the Ladrones of China; but, like certain places of entertainment in England, they ought to be compelled to exhibit in large letters, on their main-sails, *Licensed to carry guns, pursuant to a British act of Parliament.*"

CHAPTER XIII.

PEACE NEGOTIATIONS.—CAMPAIGN AGAINST THE CREEKS.

Condition of Affairs at the Opening of the Third Year—Congressional Appropriations—Russian Offers of Mediation—Jackson's Preparations—Battles of Emucfau, Enotachopco, and Horseshoe Bend.

AT the beginning of the third year of the war the prospects of the Americans were more discouraging than at any previous period. The European wars had come to an end for the time, Napoleon having been overthrown at Leipsic, and Great Britain, with an immense navy and an abundance of veteran troops, was at liberty to turn her entire attention upon the enemy across the Atlantic. Indeed, her fleet on our coast had been gradually increasing for several months, and Admirals Warren and Cockburn had shown a determination not to confine their operations to combats of vessel with vessel, but wherever practicable to send a force ashore to harass the people, burn their homes, and carry off their movable property. Harrison's victory was almost the only achievement of the American land forces worth mentioning. The little navy was as gallant as ever, and had suffered no defeat in

anything like an equal fight, except in the case of
the *Chesapeake;* but now it seemed likely to be
overwhelmed by a power that could send against it
a thousand war-ships. Two powerful ones had already been sent for the special purpose of capturing
one of our cruisers, the *Essex*, with orders to follow
her wherever she went, and take her at all hazards.
The operations of the privateers had struck the
English nation in its most tender spot, the pocket,
and roused it to a furious determination for ven-
geance ; while the London journals were boldly
talking of schemes for using the opportunity to cut
off various slices of our territory.

Though the Federal party had declined in popular strength, its leaders in Congress opposed the war
as bitterly as ever ; but after considerable debate an
act was passed to increase the regular army to sixty
thousand men, enlisted for five years. A bounty of
a hundred and twenty-four dollars was voted for recruits, and eight dollars to each man who brought
in one. Seven hundred men were added to the
Marine Corps, half a million dollars appropriated for
a floating battery, and a hundred dollars offered for
every prisoner brought home by a privateer. There
was a surplus of a million dollars in the treasury,
and five millions were yet to be paid in from loans,
while the revenue for the ensuing year was estimated

at ten millions.   The expenditures were estimated at forty-five millions, and Congress authorized a new loan of twenty-five millions, and a reissue of ten millions in treasury notes.

The Russian Government offered its friendly offices as a mediator for peace, three times in the course of the war ; but each time the offer was rejected by England.   Once — in March, 1813 — the offer was formally accepted on the part of the United States, and Albert Gallatin and James A. Bayard, who believed the English Government would accept it as readily, sailed for St. Petersburg, to join John Quincy Adams, American Minister at the Russian Court, in negotiating the peace. The London *Courier* probably spoke the sentiments of a large part of the British public when it said :

"We hope the Russian mediation will be refused.   Indeed, we are sure it will.   We have a love for our naval preëminence that cannot bear to have it even touched by a foreign hand.   Russia can be hardly supposed to be adverse to the principle of armed neutrality, and that idea alone would be sufficient to make us decline the offer.   We must take our stand, never to commit our naval rights to the mediation of any power.   This is the flag we must nail to the national mast, and go down rather than strike it.   The hour of concession and compromise is past. Peace must be the consequence of punishment to America ; and retraction of her insolent demands must precede negotiation. The thunder of our cannon must first strike terror into the American shores, and Great Britain must be seen and felt in all the majesty of her might, from Boston to Savannah, from the lakes of Canada to the mouths of the Mississippi."

The English Government declined the offer of mediation, as before, but expressed a willingness to nominate plenipotentiaries to make direct negotiations with the American commissioners, suggesting that the conference be held in London, unless the Americans preferred Gottenburg, Sweden. This answer was made in September, 1813, and reached the United States Government in official form in November. The President communicated it to Congress early in January, 1814, and the proposition was accepted ; Gottenburg being chosen as the place, and Henry Clay and Jonathan Russell being added to Messrs. Adams, Bayard, and Gallatin as commissioners. Their instructions were, to insist on an absolute discontinuance of the practice of search and impressment, and to offer, in consideration of this, an agreement to exclude British seamen from American vessels, and to surrender deserters.

But the best way to secure an honorable peace—

and indeed it will be the only way, until the millennium — is by exhibiting an ability to prosecute successful war. With the new appropriations, the Administration, while sending its peace commissioners abroad, prepared for more vigorous war within our own borders.

After a great deal of trouble with troops who believed their terms of service had expired, and who finally marched home in spite of all arguments and protests, Jackson, who had been made a major-general, found himself at Fort Strother in January, 1814, with nine hundred raw recruits and a few dozen men who had participated in his autumn campaign. With these and two hundred Indians he set out on a raid into the country of the Creeks.

On the 22d, near Emucfau, on Tallapoosa River, he was attacked by a large force, who made a feint on his right and then fell heavily upon his left. The General had anticipated this plan, and strengthened his left, so that after a stubborn fight the enemy were routed and pursued for three miles.

Two days later, on the return march, the troops were in the act of crossing Enotachopco Creek, when the Indians attacked again. After a few shots, the rear guard retreated in disorder, leaving not more than a hundred men to face the enemy; but these, by determined bravery, and especially by skilful use of a six-pounder with grape-shot, defeated the savages, and pursued them for two miles. Jackson himself acted as gunner. He lost in this raid about a hundred men.

In February, Jackson had a new army of five thousand men, including a regiment of United States regulars, in which Sam Houston was an ensign. The only difficulty now was with supplies ; but this was enormous. The distance from Fort Deposit to Fort Strother was only forty miles, but the roads were so bad that a wagon-train required seven days to accomplish it, though there was a horse to every barrel of flour in the load. Nearly sixty miles southeast of Fort Strother, and the same distance northeast of Montgomery, is Horseshoe Bend in the Tallapoosa, enclosing a peninsula of one hundred acres, which is less than five hundred feet wide at the neck. Here the Creek warriors, to the number of a thousand, had encamped and fortified themselves, when Jackson, with nearly three thousand men, was marching against them, for the avowed purpose of extermination. The Americans reached the place on the morning of March 27th, and Jackson sent General Coffee with the mounted men and Indians to cross the stream two miles below, countermarch, and take position on the bank in rear of the village. When he received the signal of their arrival, he moved forward with his main force, and planted two field-pieces to play upon the breastwork of logs and earth which crossed the neck of the peninsula. But a two hours' cannonade produced no effect upon it. Coffee and his Indians now crossed the river, set fire to the village, and attacked the enemy in the rear. As Jackson saw by the rising smoke what had been done, he stormed the breastwork in front, and for a little while there was desperate hand-to-hand fighting through the loop-holes. Then the troops, following the example of Major L. P. Montgomery and Ensign Houston, mounted the works, leapt down among the enemy, and plied the bayonet right and left till the Indians broke and fled. They neither asked for quarter nor received it. Whether they hid themselves in the thickets or attempted to swim the stream, they were hotly pursued, hunted out, and mercilessly shot. A portion found shelter under the bank, where felled timber and a rude breastwork protected them. Jackson summoned them to surrender, promising to spare their lives ; but they shot his messenger. After he had failed to dislodge them either by an artillery fire or a storming party, his troops set fire to the timber, and shot the Indians as they were driven out by the flames. At the close of that day, five hundred and fifty-seven

of the Creeks lay dead on the peninsula.   It is believed that not more than two hundred escaped.
One chief, Manowa, saved himself after he had been
badly wounded, by plunging into the water, holding
himself under by grasping a root, and breathing
through a reed that reached from his mouth to the
surface.   After nightfall he rose, swam the stream,
and stole away.

Jackson lost one hundred and thirty-one white
soldiers and fifty-four Cherokees.   Major Montgomery was killed, and Ensign Houston was wounded.

The savagery of this warfare is explained by the
fact that the Creeks were not fighting for any cause
of their own, real or pretended, but only as merce-
naries of the English.   In a letter written at this
time, Jackson said : " While we fight the savage,
who makes war only because he delights in blood,
and who has gotten his booty when he has scalped
his victim, we are, through him, contending against
an enemy of more inveterate character and deeper
design.   So far as my exertions can contribute, the
purposes, both of the savage and his instigator, shall
be defeated."

By these battles, the power of the Creeks was
completely broken.   Jackson compelled the remnant of the tribe to move north, and that summer
they were fed by the Government.

CHAPTER XIV.

BROWN'S CAMPAIGN ON THE NIAGARA.

The March to Buffalo—Capture of Fort Erie—Battle of Chippewa—
Brown's Plans—Battle of Lundy's Lane—Siege of Fort Erie by
the British.

COLONEL WINFIELD SCOTT, who after the failure of Wilkinson's expedition had spent a large part of the winter at Albany, arranging with Governor Tompkins the plans for the opening year, was made a brigadier-general in March, and with General Brown put the army at Plattsburg in motion for the Niagara frontier. Brown soon went to Sackett's Harbor, leaving Scott to conduct the long march alone. After passing Utica, the route lay largely through a wilderness. Where now stands Rochester, a city of a hundred thousand inhabitants, there was then but a single log house, and the scenery about the Genesee Falls, now closely hemmed in with tall buildings, was picturesque with forests and lively with rattlesnakes.

The army that assembled at Buffalo consisted of Scott's and Ripley's brigades of regulars, Porter's brigade of militia, and Hindman's battalion of regular artillery.   A camp of instruction was formed at once, the modern French system being adopted, and for three months drilling went on every day with the most rigid regularity.   The commanding General drilled the officers in squads, and they in turn drilled the men ; after which came company and battalion drills, and finally evolutions in line. It is said that Scott had but a single copy of the French work on tactics, on which all his instruction was based, and this had to be explained to the officers individually, most of whom were not able to read French.

Late in June, General Brown reached Buffalo, and a campaign across the river was planned at once. Early in the morning of July 3d the troops of Scott and Hindman crossed the Niagara from Black Rock, landing below Fort Erie, while Ripley's crossed a little later and landed above the fort.   The work was invested, and after the exchange of a few shots, by which four Americans and one man of the garrison were killed, it surrendered.   A hundred and seventy men were made prisoners and sent across the river.

The main body of the British forces, commanded by General Riall, was at Chippewa, on the bank of the Niagara just above the great falls, about sixteen miles below Fort Erie.   A detachment, commanded by Lieutenant-Colonel Pearson, had been thrown forward as a corps of observation nearly to the fort.

On the 4th of July the Americans marched on Chippewa. Scott's brigade, starting in the morning, led the van, and had a running fight the whole sixteen miles with Pearson's detachment. That officer afterward remarked that he was surprised at the vigor of the pursuit, and could not account for it till he remembered what day it was. When they arrived at Chippewa River, it was nightfall, and Pearson crossed it and joined Riall. Scott rested for the night on the south bank of Street's Creek, which is two miles south of the Chippewa. These two streams flow by nearly parallel courses into the Niagara, and on the plain between them the battle of Chippewa was fought next day, July 5th. Near the bank of the Niagara ran the high road. About a mile west of it was a heavy wood.

The corps of observation pursued by Scott had destroyed the bridges over the small streams as it retreated ; and it was assumed by General Brown that when he approached the Chippewa, the bridge over that stream would also be destroyed. He therefore delayed his attack while materials for a new bridge were prepared, so that when pursuit was begun it might not be interrupted. But General

Riall, as it proved, so far from contemplating retreat, determined to assume the offensive himself.

Early in the day, skirmishing began along the edge of the wood on the left, by the light troops and Indians. This at last became so annoying to the American pickets, that Porter's militia and the Indians under Red Jacket were moved through the woods still farther to the left, to flank the enemy's skirmishers. Scouts carried intelligence of this movement to Riall, and Porter's force, which began the action in good order, was soon charged by a heavy column of British regulars, before which it broke and fled.

General Brown, who had been at the front watching this movement, seeing a great cloud of dust on the left of the British lines, rode in that direction and found that Riall was pushing forward his whole force. Then he rode straight for the American rear, to hasten up Ripley's troops, who were considerably behind those of Scott. Soon after he had crossed the bridge over Strect's Creek, he met Scott, who was marching over for a dress parade on the plain. "The enemy is advancing. You will have a fight," said Brown to Scott as he passed him.

The British were already deployed in the plain, but hidden from Scott by a fringe of foliage along the creek. "Nothing but Buffalo militia!" said

Riall, as the American column came in sight, and opened his guns upon it. But when he saw them pass the bridge without wavering under a heavy fire, and deploy in order of battle, he changed his mind. "Why, these are regulars!" he exclaimed.

Towson's battery, of three guns, included in Scott's command, was planted on the high road, and the British artillery, nine pieces, had a similar position some distance to the north. Of Scott's three battalions, Major Jesup's was thrown out on the left, Major McNeil's had the centre, and Major Leavenworth's the right. The firing along the lines began at once. Seeing that by the retreat of Porter his force was likely to be flanked on the left, Scott ordered Jesup to move obliquely in that direction, and attack the extreme right of the enemy in the woods, which order Jesup's men executed, under fire, with precision and success.

The British right wing, in conflict with Jesup, became detached from the main body, whose right was thereby left exposed. Scott instantly saw his advantage and profited by it. He ordered Mc-Neil's battalion to charge obliquely upon the broken right of the main body of the enemy, and Leavenworth's at the same time to charge obliquely upon its left ; the two battalions moving as if to unite at a point behind the British line. When this movement was made, the opposing lines were within eighty paces of each other, and the firing had all the time been increasing in rapidity and destructiveness.   Two guns of Towson's battery — for one had been dismounted by a shot from the enemy's — wheeled into a position from which they could pour grape and canister through the British ranks, and their last discharge before the infantry crossed bayonets was an enfilading fire that wrought dreadful havoc.

Thus decimated by the artillery, the enemy's line soon crumbled and broke into a disorderly retreat before the steady charge of the infantry.   About the same time Jesup repelled a heavy charge by a counter charge, and the entire body of Riall's forces fled with all haste across the Chippewa, Scott's men following closely and securing some prisoners.

It was a clean victory, gained by hard fighting and skilful manœuvring ; and as the battle took place in a plain where there was scarcely any cover of any kind for the troops on either side, the losses were exceedingly heavy.   Just how many men were actually engaged, is a matter of dispute.   But on the side of the Americans the number appears not to have been over nineteen hundred, Porter's troops going out of the action before it was fairly begun, and Ripley's not arriving in time to take any part.

The number of Riall's troops in the fight appears to have been about twenty-one hundred. The loss of the Americans, in killed, wounded, and missing, was three hundred and twenty-seven ; that of the British, five hundred and three. These are the figures of the official reports, which exclude the Indians.

Riall did not tarry long to hold his position on the Chippewa. He soon sent a portion of his troops to the forts on the lower Niagara, while with the remainder he retreated to Burlington Heights. His Indian allies, eighty-seven of whom had been killed, while they had not taken a single scalp, all deserted him in disgust.

This first battle of the new campaign on the Niagara was a great inspiration to the American people, showing them that American soldiers, if properly drilled and handled, could face and defeat the best troops of the British army ; for those under Riall at Chippewa were some of the crack regiments — the Royal Scots, the King's, and the Hundredth. An English writer said : " We have now got an enemy who fights as bravely as ourselves. For some time the Americans cut no figure on land. They have now proved to us that they only wanted time to acquire a little discipline. They have now proved to us what they are made of, and they are the same sort of men as those who captured whole armies under Burgoyne and Cornwallis ; that they are neither to be frightened nor silenced ; and that if we should beat them at last, we cannot expect to do it without expending three or four hundred millions of money, keeping up all our present taxes, and adding to their amount, or imposing new taxes. These are the natural consequences of battles such as that of Chippewa."

Two days after the battle, the Americans crossed Chippewa River, and marched on Fort George. On the way, Colonel Stone, of the New York militia, burned the village of St. Davids, for which he was promptly court-martialled and dismissed from the service. Fort George was invested, and then General Brown sent to Sackett's Harbor to procure heavy guns for its reduction. But Commodore Chauncey was ill, and it seems not to have occurred to him that any other officer could command the fleet for their transportation. So Brown, unable to procure siege guns, abandoned the siege, and marched back to Queenstown, whence he sent his sick across the river, and then prepared for an active campaign.

His idea was, to move against Burlington Heights and capture them, then continue his march along the northern shore of the lake and capture York,

and thence, still following the lake shore, march on
Kingston.   But for the execution of this plan he
relied upon the coöperation of Chauncey's fleet, and
that he soon found he was not likely to have.

On the 24th of July he continued his retreat to
Chippewa, with the hope of drawing out Riall.   In
the afternoon of the 25th he received information
that the enemy had thrown a thousand men across
the Niagara, from Queenstown to Lewiston.   Supposing they intended to capture the magazine at
Schlosser and intercept supplies coming from Buffalo, General Brown determined to draw them back
if possible by again threatening the forts at the
mouth of the river.   With this purpose, he at once
sent forward General Scott with thirteen hundred
men, consisting of the battalions of Colonel Brady
and Majors Jesup, Leavenworth, and McNeil, Towson's artillery, and a detachment of cavalry under
Captain Harris.

This force, starting about five o'clock in the afternoon, marched down the road to the Falls.   As
they approached the house of a widow Wilson, near
Table Rock, several British officers were seen to
come out, mount hastily, and ride away, but not
till they had reconnoitred, through their field-
glasses, the American column.   The widow informed Scott that the officers were Riall and his

staff, and that the enemy's advance consisted of eight hundred regulars and three hundred militia, with two pieces of artillery ; the truth being that the force had nearly twice that strength.

Scott pressed forward eagerly, throwing out a part of his men to the left, and sent back word to General Brown that the enemy was in front. As the Americans emerged into a cleared field, they suddenly found themselves confronted by the British line, eighteen hundred strong, which was drawn up in Lundy's Lane, a road that starts from a point near the great Falls and runs westward. In the centre of the enemy's line was a battery of nine pieces, which occupied a rounded hillock of gentle slope just high enough to give it command of the entire field. Scott saw at once that he was in presence of a greatly superior force ; but retreat was almost impossible, and he judged it best to attack boldly, and trust to Brown for prompt reënforcement. As the Americans deployed in line of battle, the hostile forces were not more than a hundred and fifty paces apart, and firing began at once. The sun was now less than an hour high.

Towson's three guns made a gallant fight, but could effect little against the nine guns of the enemy, which were served rapidly and skilfully. The British left was east of the road that skirted the river, and was separated from the rest of the line by a space of two hundred yards, which was filled with brushwood. Jesup's and Brady's commands, partly hidden by this brushwood in the twilight, attacked the detached wing, and after considerable fighting forced it back upon the centre, capturing General Riall and several officers of his staff, after which Jesup and Brady resumed their place in the line. At the same time, the British right wing, which was longer than the American left, was thrown forward in an attempt to envelop it. To meet this danger, Scott sent McNeil's battalion against it, and after severe fighting, with heavy losses, the enemy's flanking movement was frustrated.

Both the messenger sent back by Scott and the sound of the guns announced to General Brown what was going on, and he ordered Ripley's brigade and Porter's volunteers to advance and join in the action. At the report of the first gun, Ripley had put his men in marching order, and when the word came to move they moved without a minute's delay. General Brown rode before them to the battle-field, and by the time of their arrival it was dark. About the same time, the enemy also was reënforced.

Ripley's brigade formed on Scott's right, and joined in the battle, which had not in the least abated at the departure of daylight. He soon saw that the strength of the enemy lay in the destructive battery that crowned the hill in the centre, and called upon Colonel James Miller, of the Twenty-first Regiment, to take it. " I'll try, Sir," was the now famous answer of Miller, who at once put his men in motion toward the battery. They crept silently up to a fence at the foot of the slope, put their muskets softly through it, took deliberate aim at the gunners, who had lighted matches in their hands, and at a whispered command fired in volley, shooting down every one of them. Miller's men then rose, pushed the fence flat upon the ground, rushed forward, and cleared the hill of the enemy. Meanwhile Scott's men, obstinately holding their first position, had kept on steadily firing, receiving as constant a fire in return, and both inflicted and suffered heavy loss. McNeil's battalion, having lost its commander and every one of its captains, and fired away all its ammunition, retired from the field ; and a little later, Colonel Brady being disabled, his regiment also retired for a similar reason. But a considerable number of the men of these two commands joined themselves to the regiments that still stood firm, and reëntered the fight.

After Miller's capture of the battery, the American line was re-formed, nearly at right angles to its former position, facing west, and advanced so as to hold the ground occupied by the battery. The enemy also formed a new line, and for two hours made the most desperate efforts to re-take the guns. There was constant firing, aim being taken by the flashes along the opposing lines, and more than once the bayonets were crossed in bloody hand-to-hand work in the darkness. It is said that at one time the continuous blaze of the cannon and small arms made that part of the field almost as light as day. During the struggle, both parties were re-enforced by fresh troops, but Ripley's men firmly held the ground, repelling every attack, till the enemy gave it up and retired.

General Brown and General Scott were both wounded, and the command devolved upon General Ripley, who, an hour after the enemy had retired, withdrew the entire American force from the field, carrying off the wounded, and before morning was in camp at Chippewa. As all the artillery horses had been killed, the guns for which so costly a struggle had been made were left where they stood, and of course they fell into the hands of the enemy when he returned next morning and encamped on the deserted battle-ground. The principal reason why the Americans abandoned the field was, the want of water.

The whole number of Americans engaged in this battle was about two thousand six hundred ; the whole number of British, about four thousand five hundred. The American loss was one hundred and seventy-four killed, five hundred and sixty-five wounded, and one hundred and five missing — almost one third of the entire force. Among the killed or mortally wounded were Colonel Brady and Majors Leavenworth, McNeil, and McFarland. The British loss was eighty-four killed, five hundred and fifty-seven wounded, and two hundred and thirty-five missing or prisoners. The action has been called the Battle of Niagara, and the Battle of Bridgewater, but the most commonly accepted name is Battle of Lundy's Lane.

Ripley soon afterward destroyed the bridge over the Chippewa, and retired toward Buffalo. By Brown's orders, the troops were thrown into Fort Erie, where they were reënforced, and General Ripley was superseded by General Edmund P. Gaines.

As soon as he was able to move, General Drummond, who had succeeded to the command of the British forces, marched on Fort Erie. A detachment which he sent across the river to attack Buffalo was met and defeated at Black Rock, but a party in boats captured two of Perry's vessels which were moored under the guns of the fort.

At midnight on the 14th of August, the enemy, who had been busy for two weeks planting batteries and occasionally bombarding the works, attempted to carry them by storm. The Americans were expecting the attack, and the preparations for making it were not more careful and elaborate than those for receiving it. The flints were withdrawn from the British muskets, both to insure silence in the approach and because General Drummond had issued a secret order in which he "strongly recommended a free use of the bayonet," and after dark a great number of scaling-ladders were carried forward and placed in convenient positions. The Americans had their guns charged with grape and canister, dark lanterns burning, and every musket at hand and ready for immediate use. At one battery, for lack of canister, bags were made of tent-cloth, filled with musket-balls, and loaded into the guns.

The storming party was in three columns. That which assaulted the American left, where Towson's battery was placed, marched up in the face of a continuous blaze of artillery and musketry, and, in spite of the storm of shot that rolled through it, tried to scale the defences, and actually crossed bayonets with the defenders. But in vain. Four such assaults were made by this column, and all were bloodily repelled. The rapidity with which the guns of the American battery were served, making an almost constant flash, gave it the name of "Towson's lighthouse."

On the right of the American works a similar assault was made at the same time by another column, which was met in a similar way. Major Douglass filled his guns to the muzzle with the bags of musket-balls, and though his cannoneers could not distinctly see their enemies, they were so familiar with the contour of the ground in front that they knew how to sweep it as effectively as if it had been broad daylight. Here also the attack failed.

The central column was a little more successful. The assailants dashed forward with their scaling-ladders, and mounted the parapet of the main fort, but were met at the edge by the Americans, who in a bloody fight hand-to-hand hurled them back. Three times this was repeated, with the same result. The column then moved silently around to another point, put up the ladders again, and mounted so quickly as to get a foothold within the bastion before the Americans could rally in sufficient force at the new point of attack to prevent them. Their commander, Lieutenant-Colonel Drummond, was at their head, and repeatedly called out to his men to "give the Yankees no quarter." Troops were

TOWSON'S LIGHTHOUSE

rapidly drawn to this point from other parts of the fort, and here the bloodiest work of the night was done. The highest officers present mingled personally in the fray. Lieutenant McDonough, an American, being badly wounded, asked for quarter, which Drummond refused, at the same time repeating his order to his men to refuse it in all cases. McDonough roused himself for one more effort, seized a handspike, and kept several assailants at bay, till Drummond disabled him with a pistol-shot. An American who saw this at once shot Colonel Drummond through the breast, and followed the shot with a bayonet-thrust. The Colonel had in his pocket a copy of General Drummond's secret order, and the bayonet passed through the sentence in which "a free use of the bayonet" was recommended.*

At daylight the enemy still held the bastion he had gained in the night, and several determined attempts to dislodge him failed, though the number of men he had thrown into it was being continually reduced by an irregular fire directed upon it. The British reserve was now brought up to reënforce the party in the bastion, while Douglass turned the guns of his battery so as to sweep diagonally the

----

* This blood-stained document is now in the possession of the New York Historical Society.

ground over which it must pass, and Fanning's battery was already playing upon the enemy with considerable effect. But at the moment when the reserves were ready to make a rush for the bastion, there was a tremendous explosion, and the platform of the bastion, with all the men upon it, was hurled into the air. Masses of earth, stones, broken timbers, and dead and living bodies of men rose two hundred feet, and in falling were scattered to a great distance. It was a chest of ammunition that had exploded ; but how it happened is unknown. Some of the American officers present believed it to be purely accidental, others said that Lieutenant McDonough, lying wounded at the foot of the bastion, being exasperated at the treatment he had received, applied the match and sacrificed himself for the sake of defeating his barbarous foe. The British reserves at once fell back, the contest was abandoned, and the shattered columns returned to their camp. According to General Drummond's official report, his loss in killed, wounded, and missing, was nine hundred and five. But as he gives the number of his killed as only fifty-eight, while the Americans found two hundred and twenty-two British soldiers dead on the field, it may be that even his acknowledged total loss of nearly a thousand is an understatement. The Americans lost eighty-four, besides forty-five men disabled by the cannonade that preceded the night assault.

General Gaines set to work at once to rebuild the ruined bastion and strengthen the whole line of works, while the enemy, after receiving reënforcements, began a siege by regular approaches. They soon brought their parallels so close that they were able to throw shells and hot shot into the fort every day. One shell descended through the roof of General Gaines's headquarters, and exploded at his feet, so injuring him that he was forced to give up the command to General Brown, and retire to Buffalo. The Americans in the fort, as well as the besiegers, had been reënforced, and General Brown planned a grand sortie to break up the siege works. The enemy's camp was two miles in the rear, and one third of his force was thrown forward at a time to work on the parallels. The Americans secretly marked out a road through the woods, leading from their left around to a point close upon the right of the besiegers. On the 17th of September two columns, of about one thousand men each, sallied out from the fort. One column followed the road through the woods and suddenly burst upon the British right, while the other marched through a ravine, against the centre. Before reënforcements could come from the British camp, the Americans leaped into the siege works, after bloody fighting overcame all resistance, dismounted the guns and rendered them useless, exploded the magazines, and returned to the fort with many prisoners. This operation cost the Americans five hundred and twenty men, killed, wounded, or missing, and the British six hundred and nine.

In the night of the 21st, General Drummond raised the siege, and retired beyond the Chippewa. In October the Americans dismantled Fort Erie, and returned to the eastern shore of the Niagara.

CHAPTER XV.

THE SECOND INVASION OF NEW YORK.

Fight at La Colle Mill—Ship-building—Yeo's Attack on Oswego—
Affairs at Charlotte and Poultneyville—Fight at Sandy Creek—
Izard's Failure on the Niagara—Expedition against Michilimacki-
nac—Prevost's Advance into New York—Its Purpose—Battle of
Plattsburg.

In February General Wilkinson had removed his
army from French Mills to Plattsburg, on Lake
Champlain, and a month later he added one more
to the futile invasions of Canada. At the head of
four thousand men, he crossed the border, March
30th, met a party of British at Odelltown, with
whom skirmishing was carried on for three miles
along the road, and found the enemy seriously in
his path at La Colle Mill, on the Sorel, four miles
from Rouse's Point, where about two hundred men
were posted in a stone mill and a block-house, on
either side of La Colle Creek.

Wilkinson brought up two pieces of artillery and
planted them within two hundred yards of the stone
mill. Then he disposed his forces in such a way as
nearly to surround it and cut off the retreat of the
enemy when his guns should knock the walls of the

mill about their heads.   But though the guns were served with great skill and rapidity for two hours, the walls would n't budge, and it did not occur to the enemy to attempt a retreat.   On the contrary, from their secure position they used their rifles so effectively that Wilkinson's men suffered severely. Captain McPherson, commanding the battery, was wounded in the chin, but tied it up with his handkerchief and remained at his post till another shot broke his thigh, when he was borne off.   His successor, Lieutenant Larrabee, was soon shot through the lungs, when he also was borne to the rear ; and Lieutenant Sheldon then kept the battery in play till the close of the fight.

Major Hancock, commanding the enemy, having received reënforcements that swelled the number of his men to about a thousand, ordered a sortie, to capture the battery.   His troops suddenly burst from the mill, and made a rush for the guns.   But this subjected them to a fire from the American infantry, by which they suffered heavily, and they were obliged to return to the mill and the blockhouse.   A second and more desperate sortie had the same result, and the enemy then shut themselves up in the house and defied all attempts to drive them out.   As the condition of the roads prevented him from bringing up heavier artillery, Wilkinson gave up the expedition and returned through mud, snow, and rain to Plattsburg. The affair had cost him a hundred and fifty-four men, and inflicted on the enemy a loss of sixty-one. The General asked for a court-martial, and was tried and acquitted ; but this ended his military career. General George Izard succeeded to his command.

Both belligerents were still building ships for service on Lake Ontario. The British had a large one on the stocks at Kingston, and the Americans an equally large one at Sackett's Harbor. All sorts of insignificant affairs took place during the spring and summer along the shores of this lake and Lake Champlain, effecting nothing, but keeping the people in a state of alarm.

On one occasion three boats approached Sackett's Harbor, carrying two barrels of powder, with which it was intended to blow up the new vessel on the stocks. But they were discovered and fired at, whereupon the crews hastily threw the powder overboard, fearing it would be exploded by a bullet, and pulled away.

Finding that he could not destroy the new ship, Sir James Yeo determined to render her useless by capturing the guns, rigging, and stores intended for her, which were at Oswego. Accordingly he organized an expedition of about three thousand men, the troops being commanded by General Drummond, and sailed for that place early in May. The fort at Oswego, an old affair, in a dilapidated condition, was on one side of the river, and the village on the other. Lieutenant-Colonel Mitchell, commanding at the fort, saw the approaching expedition early in the morning of May 5th. As his force was too small to be divided, he sent a large number of tents across the river, and had them pitched in front of the village. This convinced the enemy that there was a heavy force on that side of the river, and he confined his attention to the fort.

The ships bombarded the work, and a force attempted to land by means of boats. But Colonel Mitchell sent a few men down the shore with one old gun, and as soon as they came within range it made such havoc among the boats' crews that they pulled back to the fleet. One of the boats, sixty feet long, propelled by three sails and thirty-six oars, was so shattered that it was abandoned and drifted ashore.

The next day the fleet returned to the attack, and this time succeeded in landing about two thousand men. Colonel Mitchell, who had been reënforced by a small body of militia, gradually retired before the invaders, making a gallant resistance as long as it was of any use, and then retreated to a point several miles up the river, whither most of the stores had been removed, and destroyed the bridges behind him. The enemy raised and carried away the schooner *Growler*, which, as it contained some of the guns for the new vessel, the Americans had sunk on the approach of the expedition; burned the barracks, took whatever he could find that was movable, and on the 7th sailed away. The action had cost him two hundred and thirty-five men, killed, wounded, or drowned. The Americans had lost sixty-nine.

Five days later a British squadron appeared before Charlotte, at the mouth of Genesee River. The village was guarded by sixty men, with one field-piece. Word was sent to General Peter B. Porter, who arrived on the morning of the 13th, just in time to refuse a demand for the surrender of the place. Two gunboats then entered the river and bombarded the town for an hour and a half, throwing in shells, rockets, and round shot. The women and children were removed, a militia force of three hundred and fifty men was collected, and dispositions were made to capture the boats if they should venture farther up the river. A second demand for a surrender, with a threat to land twelve hundred men and destroy the village, was refused by Porter, and on the 15th the boats bombarded the place again for some hours, and then withdrew.

In the evening the squadron sent a force on shore at Poultneyville, where some stores were captured ; but a small body of militia under General John Swift soon appeared and drove the enemy precipitately back to their boats.

As Sir James Yeo was blockading Sackett's Harbor for the special purpose of preventing the armament of the new vessel from being carried in, the wits of the Americans were taxed to get the guns and cables there. Transportation all the way by land would have been tedious and costly. The task was assigned to Captain Woolsey, of the navy. He caused a story to be circulated, in a way that made it sure to reach the vigilant enemy, that the guns were to be transported by way of Oneida Lake. They were on nineteen boats, and on the 28th of May he ran the rapids and arrived at Oswego with them at dusk. The plan was, to coast along down the lake as far as Sandy Creek, eight miles from Sackett's Harbor, run up the creek, and thence carry them overland. Accompanied by a hundred and twenty riflemen, under Major Appling, the flotilla went down the lake by night as far as Big Salmon River, and in the morning one boat was missing. At this point a body of Oneida Indians joined the expedition, and at noon on the 29th it reached Sandy Creek. The missing boat had gone on to Sackett's Harbor, where — perhaps purposely — it fell into the hands of the blockaders, to whom its crew told the whole story of Woolsey's flotilla. Sir James at once sent a force, in two gunboats and four smaller craft, to capture it. This expedition sailed up Sandy Creek on the morning of the 30th, thinking to make sure prize of the flotilla and its cargo of guns and cables. But Major Appling had placed his riflemen in ambush along the bank, and near the flotilla was Captain Melville with a company of light artillery and two six-pounders. The enemy's gunboats opened fire on the flotilla as fast as they came within gunshot, and a party of troops was landed. As soon as they were within range of Appling's rifles, he poured in a deadly fire upon their flank and rear, while at the same time the artillery played upon them in front. In ten minutes the British lost eighteen men killed and fifty wounded, when the whole force surrendered. The captured boats mounted seven guns, and there were a hundred and sixty-five prisoners. The Americans had two men wounded. The Indians took no active part in the fight.

This affair inflicted so serious a loss upon the British fleet that it returned to Kingston, and remained there till another ship and more men could be obtained. The Americans arrived safely at

Sackett's Harbor with their guns, and the new frigate, the *Mohawk*, was launched on the 11th of June. Chauncey's squadron then consisted of nine vessels, mounting two hundred and fifty-one guns.

Early in August, General Izard, being ordered to relieve General Brown in the command on the Niagara frontier, marched from Plattsburg with about four thousand troops, leaving General Alexander Macomb in command there with twelve hundred, including the invalids. After his arrival at Buffalo, Izard crossed the Niagara with about eight thousand men, and set forward to attack Drummond on the Chippewa. But the British commander, after one sharp skirmish, withdrew his forces to Fort George and Burlington Heights. Izard, who lacked the energy to follow, persuaded himself, in spite of the almanac, that the season was far advanced, and retired to Black Rock.

Another American expedition on the upper lakes was not more satisfactory or creditable in its result. It was intended for the re-capture of Michilimackinac, the first place taken by the British during the war. The garrison was strengthened in April, 1814, and three months later a detachment sent out from it captured the American post at Prairie du Chien.

The naval portion of the expedition was entrusted to Commander Arthur St. Clair, who had five vessels which had formed part of Perry's fleet. He took on board five hundred regular troops and about the same number of militia, commanded by Lieutenant-Colonel Croghan, who had made the gallant defence of Fort Stephenson the year before, sailed on the 12th of July, and arrived at Michili-mackinac on the 26th. There was a difference of opinion as to the best mode of attack; St. Clair was unwilling to attempt it first with his vessels, because the fort was so far above the water that it could send a plunging fire upon their decks.

On the 4th of August the troops were landed on the north side of the island, to attack the fort in the rear. But Lieutenant-Colonel McDonall, who commanded it, had drawn out his entire garrison, and taken up a strong position in the path of the Americans. His men were behind a small ridge which formed a natural breastwork, the ground in front was perfectly clear, and two field-pieces commanded it. On each of their flanks was a thick wood, and in these woods McDonall posted a force of Indians. Croghan advanced with his militia in front, and attempted to turn the British left. But a volley from the Indians in the woods, whom he had not discovered, killed Major Holmes, wounded Captain Desha, and threw the American right wing into confusion. Croghan then attacked the enemy's centre, and drove him from his breastwork into the woods in his rear. But beyond this point it seemed impossible to accomplish anything, and the Americans soon withdrew from the field and reëmbarked. They had lost thirteen men killed, fifty-two wounded, and two missing. The British loss is unknown.

But while these insignificant actions were taking place along the whole length of the lakes, a serious danger threatened the country at the eastern extremity of that line, and was averted by a brilliant victory.

The British troops at the foot of Lake Champlain had been heavily reënforced by veterans from the armies that had conquered Napoleon, and Sir George Prevost, who had been ordered to make an invasion of New York by the route taken by Burgoyne in 1777, seized the opportunity when the Americans at Plattsburg were weakened by the absence of Izard and the four thousand men he had taken with him to the Niagara frontier.

The object of the movement was, to capture and hold a portion of the State of New York; so that when the pending peace negotiations were brought to a close, it might be stipulated that all territory should remain with the party in whose possession it then was, and this would give the English complete control of the St. Lawrence and Lake Champlain, if not of Lake Ontario also. In accordance with this purpose, Prevost issued a proclamation to the inhabitants of that sparsely settled region, calling upon them to renounce allegiance to the United States, renew their allegiance to Great Britain, and furnish his troops subsistence. Had his forces been victorious, he would have claimed that this had been done, and the English would then probably have been successful in their purpose to "change the boundary of New York."

General Alexander Macomb, who had been left in command at Plattsburg on the departure of General Izard, and had been told by that officer that he must expect to be driven out or made a prisoner by the enemy, had made up his mind to falsify the prediction, and exhibited wonderful energy in putting the place into a defensible condition.

Saranac River, after running parallel with the shore of Lake Champlain for a short distance, turns sharply to the east and flows into Cumberland or Plattsburg Bay. On the peninsula thus enclosed, which is about half a mile wide, the Americans constructed three redoubts and two block-houses, one of them being at the mouth of the river. The north bank is about thirty feet high ; and the south bank, which was the one occupied by the Americans, about fifty.   Macomb had fifteen hundred regulars, and two thousand militia.

Prevost, with fourteen thousand troops, began his advance on the 29th of August, crossed the border on the 1st of September, and thenceforth found his march impeded somewhat by felled trees and broken bridges.   He was in no great hurry, however, as he was in advance of the fleet, commanded by Commodore George Downie, on whose coöperation he relied.   He impressed the horses of farmers along the route for the transportation of his artillery and supplies, and arrived before Plattsburg on the 6th.   The advance of his right column was assaulted by a small body of riflemen under Major John E. Wool, who inflicted some loss and drove it back upon the main body.   Wool fell back, was joined by Captain Leonard's battery, made another stand, inflicted more loss with the artillery, and again fell back slowly till he crossed the Saranac, destroying the bridge behind him.   The enemy's left column, approaching by a road nearer the lake, was annoyed by skirmishers under Lieutenant-Colonel Appling, and by the American gun-boats.   Both bridges were destroyed, and when the enemy's riflemen posted themselves in several houses on the north bank, these were set on fire by hot shot.

But the British fleet had not yet come up, and

Prevost, while waiting for it, spent several days in erecting batteries and perfecting his preparations for a serious assault. The fleet appeared on the morning of the 11th, and the General gave orders for an immediate advance.

His men attempted to ford the river at three places — where the two bridges had been, and at a point farther up, known as Pike's Cantonment — their movements being covered by a heavy fire from the British batteries. The troops that actually advanced to the assault numbered eight thousand, and they carried an immense number of scaling-ladders, to enable them to climb the high bank and afterward surmount the American works.

At the lower bridge, the fire from the forts and block-houses drove them back. At the upper bridge, they were prevented from landing by a steady fire of musketry. At Pike's Cantonment, where the river was easily fordable, there was only militia to dispute the passage. Yet several attempts to cross were repelled ; and when finally a body of regulars succeeded in crossing, the militia rallied and drove it back again with heavy loss. At this point of time the issue of the battle had been decided by the action on the water.

The American flotilla, commanded by Lieutenant Thomas Macdonough, was drawn up in line to await the attack, in such manner that the British ships could not enter the bay without being exposed to a broad-side fire.   Macdonough's vessels were all stationed with their prows to the north, the *Eagle*, of twenty guns, at the head of the line; then the *Saratoga*, flag-ship, of twenty-six guns; then the *Ticonderoga*, of seventeen; and lastly the *Preble*, of seven, which was so near a shoal that the enemy could not pass around her.   Macdonough also had ten galleys or gun-boats, which he placed inside of his line, opposite the intervals between the larger vessels.   The British flotilla also consisted of four large vessels — carrying respectively thirty-seven, sixteen, eleven, and eleven guns — and twelve gun-boats.   The total American force was fourteen vessels, with eighty-six guns and eight hundred and fifty men; the total British force, sixteen vessels, with ninety-five guns and one thousand and fifty men.

The peculiar thing in Macdonough's preparations, and the one perhaps which secured him the victory, was an arrangement by which he made it possible to turn his flag-ship almost instantly so as to bring her broadside to bear on any point.   He did this by laying a kedge anchor broad off each of her bows, and carrying the hawsers to the quarters.   Thus by winding in one or the other of the hawsers the stern of the ship could be swung one way or the other, while the cable of the main anchor kept her bow in one place.

The English line bore down upon the American in fine style, the first two vessels firing as they approached. The flag-ship *Confiance* did not open fire till she had dropped anchor within a quarter of a mile of her foe.

The *Eagle*, at the head of the American line, began firing in a wild way, without orders, before her shot could reach the enemy. The excitement was soon felt through the fleet, and was shared by a young cock which had escaped from his coop on the deck of the *Saratoga*. In response to the boom of the cannon, he flew upon a gun-slide, flapped his wings, and crowed loudly. The sailors burst into a hearty laugh, and gave three cheers. Then a long gun, sighted by Macdonough himself, was fired, and as the shot raked the deck of the *Confiance*, the whole line opened and the battle became general. The first broadside from the *Confiance* disabled forty men on the *Saratoga ;* for fifteen minutes everything was ablaze, and the roar was continuous. Then the vessel at the head of the British line struck her colors.

The enemy's shot cut away the *Eagle's* springs — ropes fastened either to the anchor or to the cable, and passed to the quarter, in order to sway the ship to one side or the other and bring the guns to bear on any desired point. Her commander, Lieutenant Henley, then cut his cable, sheeted home the topsails, ran down behind the *Saratoga*, and took a position between her and the *Ticonderoga*, anchoring by the stern, which brought the fresh guns of his larboard battery to bear on the enemy, when they were served with good effect.

The *Preble* was attacked by the enemy's gunboats, and driven from her position ; but they were stopped by the next in line, which they vainly tried to board. Every gun of the starboard battery — the side nearest the enemy — on the American flag-ship was disabled. Then Macdonough proceeded to "wind ship," that is, to turn the vessel completely round by winding at the hawsers attached to the kedges. This was accomplished without accident, and his gunners, springing to the larboard battery, poured out fresh broadsides that made dreadful havoc with the *Confiance*. The commander of that vessel attempted to copy Macdonough's manœuvre, for her battery on the side presented to the enemy was also nearly used up, but failed, and two hours and a quarter after the fight began her colors came down. The remaining British vessels also surrendered, and the victory was complete.

When the tremendous cheer that burst from the

sailors of the American fleet announced this news, to friend and foe on shore, Sir George Prevost — who from the first had relied more upon the fleet than upon his army — gave up his whole plan, and made all haste to return to Canada.

In this bloody battle — which defeated what is known as the second invasion of New York, and preserved our territory intact — the American fleet suffered a loss of fifty-two men killed and fifty-eight wounded. The British, according to their official report, lost fifty-seven killed, including Commodore Downie, and seventy-two wounded ; Macdonough reported their loss at eighty-four killed and a hundred and ten wounded. The British galleys, before the Americans could take possession of them, drifted out into the lake, and escaped.

CHAPTER XVI.

OPERATIONS ALONG THE COAST.

Capture of Eastport and Castine—Occupation of Territory in Maine—
Destruction of the Frigate *Adams*—Bombardment of Stonington—
Affairs at Wareham, Scituate, and Boothbay.

THE close of the war in Europe had not only enabled the English to strengthen their land forces in
America, but had also liberated many of their war-
ships, and the result was felt all along our coast.
The enemy's purpose to conquer territory which
might be retained after the war, apparent enough
before, was now definitely proclaimed.

In July, Sir Thomas Hardy, commander of the
British fleet before New London, received orders to
capture Moose Island, in Passamaquoddy Bay, and
sailed thither with five ships of war and transports
containing about fifteen hundred troops. The
Americans had here a small fort, garrisoned by
only fifty men, under Major Putnam, who made
no resistance to the enemy, but surrendered at once,
July 11th. Sir Thomas then took formal possession
not only of the town of Eastport, which at that
time contained about one thousand inhabitants, but

of the whole island, and issued a proclamation in which he declared that all the islands in the bay had been surrendered and were thenceforth British territory. He gave the inhabitants one week in which to make their choice, either to swear allegiance to the British Crown or move away. About two thirds of the people took the oath, supposing they would thereby be admitted to the privileges of British citizenship ; but a month later the Provincial Council of New Brunswick ordered that they should be treated as a conquered province and placed under martial law. The fortifications of Eastport were greatly strengthened, the six guns being increased to sixty, and a large garrison placed there. But provisions were extremely scarce, the men deserted in great numbers, and the British officers were often seen on the ramparts, doing duty as sentinels.

On the 1st of September, another British force entered Penobscot River. The small American garrison at Castine blew up the fort and retreated, and the enemy took possession, and soon issued a proclamation declaring all that part of Maine east of the Penobscot to be conquered territory. It contained about forty villages, with an aggregate of more than thirty thousand inhabitants.

Captain Morris, after a successful cruise, had recently arrived in the Penobscot with the American frigate *Adams*, and taken her to Hampden, thirty-five miles up the river, for repairs. The British commander sent up an expedition of about a thousand men to capture her, and Captain Morris made all possible preparations for defence. He erected several batteries on the shore, collected a small force of militia from the neighborhood, and, as they were unarmed, put the ship's muskets into their hands. But on the approach of the British regulars, the militia ran away; and Morris, seeing that he could not save his vessel, sent away his sailors and marines, who retreated across a bridge over a deep creek. He and a few men whom he had retained for the service then set a slow-match to the magazine, and, as their retreat by the bridge had been cut off, swam the stream and escaped. The frigate was blown to pieces, and the enemy returned to Castine with neither prisoners nor plunder. But they made thenceforth frequent incursions among the towns of the neighborhood, and freely robbed the inhabitants of what little property they had that was worth taking.

The next orders issued to the British Commodore, Sir Thomas Hardy, were to destroy the town of Stonington, Connecticut ; which he found a very different task from the capture of Moose Island. With two frigates, a brig, and a bomb-vessel, he appeared before the town on the 9th of August, and sent in word that he should begin a bombardment in one hour. The women and children were hastily removed, and the men repaired to the defences of the place. These consisted of a small breastwork and three pieces of artillery — two eighteen-pounders, and a six-pounder. A rude flag-staff was erected, and a small flag nailed to it. Those who had been trained as artillerists took their places at the guns, and the remainder, with muskets, were placed behind the breastwork. Word was sent to General Cushing, commanding at New London, and couriers on horseback rode through the surrounding country to rally the militia.

It was toward evening when Hardy opened his ports and fired upon the town every kind of missile in use at that day — round-shot, grape-shot, canister, bomb-shells, carcasses, rockets, and stink-pots. A carcass was a cylindrical cage or framework of iron, covered with canvas and filled with combustibles, intended to set the buildings on fire. About eight o'clock, while the bombardment was still going on, five barges and a launch filled with men and carrying several guns approached the shore. The Americans permitted them to come within close range, and then poured such a fire of grape-shot into them from the two eighteen-pounders that they were very soon compelled to retire. They then sailed around to the eastern side of the little peninsula, where they supposed it was defenceless. But the Americans dragged the six-pounder across, and were ready for them. With this gun alone, so rapidly was it served and so skilfully handled, they again drove off the fleet of barges.

The bombardment was kept up till midnight, and next day the fleet was increased by the arrival of another brig. The vessels now took a position nearer the shore, and the action was reopened. One brig was anchored within pistol-shot of the battery, at which it directed its guns. But the old eighteen-pounders sent several balls through her between wind and water, compelling her to haul off and repair damages. The barges made an attempt to land a force, as on the day before ; but met a similar reception and once more retired. One of the barges was completely torn to pieces by the fire of the six-pounder. The fleet then drifted out of reach of the battery, but kept up the bombardment at long range during that and the following day. On the 12th, Sir Thomas, who had lost twenty-one men killed and more than fifty wounded, bore up and sailed away.

Of the Americans, six had been slightly wounded, and one mortally. Of the hundred houses in Stonington, forty had been more or less injured, ten of them badly, and two or three were entirely destroyed. The enemy had thrown in more than sixty tons of metal. Colonel Randall, the commanding officer, received high praise for the manner in which he had conducted the defence, as did also Lieutenants Lathrop and Hough.

There were smaller affairs of the same nature, at various points along the New England coast. At Wareham the enemy landed in safety by means of a flag of truce, and then burned a large cotton factory and the vessels at their moorings. At Scituate also they burned the shipping. But at Boothbay the militia rallied and drove them off with considerable loss. The attempt to land was repeated on several different days, but every time without success.

CHAPTER XVII.

THE WASHINGTON CAMPAIGN.

Ross's Expedition against Washington—Battle of Bladensburg—Destruction of the Capital—Capitulation of Alexandria—Comments of the London *Times*—Expedition against Baltimore—Death of Sir Peter Parker—Battle of North Point—Death of General Ross—Bombardment of Fort McHenry—How a Famous Song was written.

BUT these little affairs along the coast were of small consequence in comparison with what befell the capital of the country. Relieved by the peace in Europe, the English Government resolved to prosecute the American war with greater vigor, and fixed upon the policy of striking at the cities. Baltimore, Washington, Charleston, Savannah, and New Orleans were all marked for capture or destruction. A powerful British fleet was sent to the Bermudas, and a large number of veteran troops transported thither, and the commanders on our coasts were directed to draw thence such forces as they might need for their expeditions.

That Washington was likely to be the object of a hostile demonstration of some kind, was known to the Administration for months, but no efficient measures were taken to meet it. President Madison and General Armstrong, Secretary of War, did not like each other, and neither man was large enough not to let his personal feelings stand in the way of the country's interests. When the President urged that something should be done to avert the danger that threatened the capital, General Armstrong opposed the proposition with such abstruse reasons as that "militia were always most effective when first called out."

The only effective means of defence consisted of a small flotilla commanded by Commodore Joshua Barney, who sailed the waters of Chesapeake Bay for some weeks, continually annoying the English fleet. On the 1st of June he had an engagement with two schooners in the Patuxent, and drove them off with hot shot. A few days later, he was chased into St. Leonard's Creek, where he formed his boats in line of battle across the channel and engaged the enemy's barges, ultimately chasing them down to the ships. On the 10th he was attacked by twenty barges and two schooners ; but he beat them all off, and so severely handled one of the schooners, an eighteen-gun vessel, that her crew ran her aground and abandoned her. On the 26th, with the help of a corps of artillery and a detachment of the marine corps, Barney attacked the whole squadron that was blockading him in the St. Leonard's, and after a fight of two hours compelled them to raise the blockade.

General Robert Ross, who had served in several campaigns under Wellington, and was with Sir John Moore when he fell at Corunna, was selected by the Duke to command an expedition against Washington. In July, with three thousand five hundred men, the finest regiments of Wellington's army, he sailed from Bordeaux for the Chesapeake, where he arrived in August, and was at once reënforced by a thousand marines from Cockburn's blockading squadron, and a hundred negroes from the neighboring plantations, who had been armed and drilled as British soldiers.

The District of Columbia and the adjacent counties of Virginia and Maryland had recently been formed into a military district, of which the command was given to General William H. Winder. His forces consisted of five hundred regulars and two thousand militia. On the approach of the enemy, Maryland and Virginia were hastily called upon for reënforcements of militia, and nearly three thousand came from Maryland; but the Virginians, from delay in receiving their flints, did not move till the fighting was over.

Ross's expedition ascended the Patuxent, and on

the morning of August 19th his troops were debarked without molestation at Benedict, on the western or right bank, forty miles southeast of Washington. He had twenty-seven vessels, and over four thousand men.

By order of the Secretary of War, Commodore Barney blew up his little flotilla, and with his five hundred seamen and marines retreated to Nottingham, where General Winder assigned to them the management of the artillery.

The weather was fearfully hot, and the enemy proceeded by slow marches, dozens of men falling and fainting by the way. It was remarked at the time that their route might have been so impeded by felling trees, that the weather and the labor of removing them would have defeated the expedition. But nothing of the sort was done. Winder waited in a chosen position at Wood Yard, twelve miles from the city, to give battle. But Ross turned to the right after reaching Nottingham, taking the road to Marlborough, where Admiral Cockburn joined him with a body of marines and seamen. The Americans fell back to Battalion Old Fields, a detachment under Major Peters skirmishing sharply with the advancing enemy, and on the 24th to Bladensburg, six miles from Washington, where a bridge spanned the eastern branch of the

Potomac.   Here they made a stand, taking a strong position on the western bank, commanding the bridge.   The President and several members of his Cabinet were on the field, all interfering more or less with the military arrangements.   Monroe — then Secretary of State, afterward President — who had been a staff officer in the Continental army more than thirty years before, considered himself specially qualified as a military meddler, and actually changed the disposition of some of Winder's troops at the last moment.

It could not be expected that a mass of raw militia, hastily called together, and hardly knowing, by whom they were commanded, would stand long, even in an advantageous position, before the onset of veteran troops.   "Come, General Armstrong, come, Colonel Monroe," said the President, "let us go, and leave it to the commanding General."   So Mr. Madison and his Cabinet left the field, and it was not long before the militia followed their illustrious example.

The ground on the eastern side of the river, where the British approached, was low and clear. On the western it rose in a gradual slope, and along the stream was fringed with willows and larches. A body of American riflemen was posted in the shrubbery that lined the bank.   Three hundred yards up the slope was a slight earthwork, mounting six guns, supported by two companies of Baltimore volunteers. General Stansbury had posted three regiments to the right of it, but Secretary Monroe had moved them to a point in the rear of the battery and five hundred yards farther up the slope. At the top of the hill, one mile from the bridge, was formed a line consisting of Maryland militia on the right, Barney's seamen and marines in the centre, a detachment of regular troops and a regiment of District militia on the left, with a battery of six guns and a company of riflemen in front.

The enemy entered the village of Bladensburg soon after noon of the 24th, and was at once subjected to a fire that compelled him to seek the shelter of the houses. At one o'clock the advance column rushed at the double quick upon the bridge, where it met a concentrated fire from the American batteries and riflemen, and almost entirely melted away. A remnant, however, succeeded in crossing, deployed at once, and advanced upon the first line, which fell back and permitted two guns to be lost.

Elated at this success, the thin line of British troops threw off their knapsacks and advanced toward the second line, without waiting for another column to cross the bridge to their support. When

General Winder saw their error, he placed himself at the head of a regiment of Baltimore volunteers, gave them an effective volley, and then made a charge, and at the point of the bayonet drove them down to the very brink of the river, where with difficulty they maintained their foothold under the trees till another brigade had crossed the bridge to their relief.

One regiment of these fresh troops turned the left of the American line, and threw in some Congreve rockets, which so frightened the militia on that flank that they broke at once and fled in confusion. The regiment headed by Winder stood firm till both its flanks were turned, when it retired, its retreat being covered by the riflemen.

The enemy then attacked the remainder of the line, all of which soon gave way, except Barney's men, who kept them in check for half an hour, and with the fire of four pieces of artillery ploughed their ranks through and through. But when the militia broke, the teamsters stampeded, without stopping to unhitch their horses from the ammunition wagons. Barney was thus left with but a single round of ammunition, while the enemy was gradually gaining a position upon his flank; and though many of his men were acting as infantry and behaved admirably, charging several times with great effect, he was obliged to order a retreat. He himself had been severely wounded, while two of his principal officers were killed, and two others wounded. He fell into the hands of the enemy, who took him to their hospital at Bladensburg. In this action the Americans had lost seventy-seven men killed or wounded ; the British, more than five hundred. Ross's entire loss, including deserters, prisoners, and those who succumbed to the weather, was said to be nearly a thousand.

But no serious obstacle now stood in the way of General Ross's purpose to destroy the capital ; and with that portion of his force which had not been engaged, he marched thither without the loss of an hour, arriving at eight o'clock that evening.

The most valuable portion of the public archives had been removed to a place of safety, and Mrs. Madison had managed to carry away the original draft of the Declaration of Independence, a portrait of Washington that hung in the White House, and a few other articles which could not have been replaced. The magazines and shipping at the Navy Yard had already been fired by order of the Secretary of War, and everything there was destroyed.

It is said that General Ross offered to spare the city for a price ; but there was no one at hand who

could treat with him, if the authorities had been inclined to purchase its safety.   He expected to be
attacked by a more formidable force than that he
had met at Bladensburg, and, as he wrote to Earl
Bathurst, "judging it of consequence to complete
the destruction of the public buildings with the
least possible delay, so that the army might retire
without loss of time," he "without a moment's
delay burned and destroyed everything in the most
distant degree connected with the government."
There was one notable exception.   At the interces-
sion of Dr. Thornton, who superintended the Patent
Office, the building containing that and the Post
Office was spared; because, as the doctor represented, it contained great numbers of models and
papers which were of value to the whole scientific
world.   The jail, one hotel, and a few dwellings
also escaped.   All else, including the President's
house, the public libraries, and the new Capitol—
of which only the wings had been built — was
given to the flames.   The commanders of the expedition distinguished themselves personally in this
vandalism.   Admiral Cochrane, who had a spite
against the *National Intelligencer* because of its
strictures upon his marauding exploits along the
coast, caused the office to be sacked and the type
thrown into the street, and with his own hand set

the building on fire. Admiral Cockburn is said to have led his men into the hall of the House of Representatives, where he leaped into the Speaker's chair and shouted, "Shall this harbor of Yankee democracy be burned? All for it will say, Aye!"

In the night of the 25th, Ross silently withdrew from the city, leaving his camp-fires burning, for he expected and feared pursuit, and marched with all that remained of his force to Benedict, where they reëmbarked.

A division of the enemy's fleet, consisting of eight vessels, ascended the Potomac to attack the city of Alexandria. Fort Warburton, a small work intended for its defence, was destroyed by the garrison at the approach of the ships, and with no opposition they passed up and laid the town under their guns. A parley was had, the result of which was that the dwellings were left unmolested, the condition being, "the immediate delivery [to the enemy] of all public and private naval and ordnance stores; of all shipping, and the furniture necessary to their equipment then in port; of all the merchandise of every description, whether in the town or removed from it since the 19th of the month; that such merchandise should be put on board the shipping at the expense of the owners; and that all vessels which might have been sunk upon the approach of the fleet should be raised by the merchants and delivered up with all their apparatus." These conditions, hard as they were, were complied with, and on the 6th of September the fleet, loaded with booty, returned down the river. Two batteries on the shore — at White House and Indian Head, commanded by Captains Porter and Perry, of the navy — damaged it considerably as it passed, but were not able to stop it.

If the importance of General Ross's exploit was overrated by the Americans, who naturally felt chagrined that so small an invading force should have destroyed their capital and momentarily dispersed their Government, it was enormously exaggerated by the English journals. By confounding the capital of the country with its metropolis, they led their readers to believe that the chief city of the United States had been laid in ashes; whereas Washington was but a straggling place of eight thousand inhabitants, which had been made the seat of the Federal Government but a dozen years before. Taking it for granted that what would have befallen England or France with London or Paris in the possession of a foreign enemy, had actually befallen the United States, the London *Times* proceeded to say: "The ill-organized association is on the eve of dissolution, and the world is speedily to be delivered of the mischievous example of the existence of a government founded on democratic rebellion." In another issue, October 9th, 1814, it said : "Next to the annihilation of the late military despotism in Europe, the subversion of that system of fraud and malignity which constitutes the whole policy of the Jeffersonian school, was an event to be devoutly wished by every man in either hemisphere who regards rational liberty or the honorable intercourse of nations. It was an event to which we should have bent, and yet must bend, all our energies. The American Government must be displaced, or it will sooner or later plant its poisoned dagger in the heart of the parent state." In a speech in Parliament, Sir Gilbert Heathcote naïvely said, "it appeared to him that we feared the rising power of America, and wished to curtail it." Which, as the Scottish captain in the story said, was "a verra just remark."

In the night of August 30th, Sir Peter Parker, commander of the frigate *Menelaus*, who had been blockading Baltimore with that and another vessel, landed on the Eastern Shore, with two hundred and thirty men, intending to surprise and capture a small body of Maryland volunteers at Moorfields. But the Maryland men were ready for them, and after a sharp fight of about an hour the British retreated, leaving sixteen of their men killed or wounded on the field, and bearing away seventeen others, among whom was Sir Peter, who died almost as soon as he reached his ship. Three of the Americans were wounded.

Rightly conjecturing that Baltimore would be the next place at which the enemy would strike, the people of that city had made haste to provide for its defence. The fortifications were extended, and manned by about five thousand men. On the 11th of September, forty British war-vessels appeared at the mouth of the Patapsco, and that night eight thousand men, under General Ross, were landed at North Point, a dozen miles below the city. No resistance was offered till they had marched four miles up the little peninsula, when they were met by General John Stricker with three thousand two hundred men, including an artillery company with six small guns, and a detachment of cavalry.

The cavalry and a hundred and fifty riflemen were thrown forward to feel the enemy. General Ross, who had declared that he " did n't care if it rained militia," and had expressed his intention of making winter quarters in Baltimore, put himself at the head of his advance guard, and promptly attacked. But as he rode along the crest of a little knoll, he was shot in the side by an American rifleman, and before his aides could bear him back to the boats, he expired.

Notwithstanding the loss of their leader, the British forces rushed steadily forward, drove the American skirmishers back upon the main line, and brought on a general engagement. The battle lasted two or three hours with varying fortune, till a heavy attack on the American left turned it, when the whole body retreated to an intrenched position near the city.

The British followed the next day, but found their enemy strongly placed and reënforced, whereupon they took advantage of a dark night and retraced their steps. They had lost two hundred and ninety men, killed or wounded, and had inflicted upon the Americans a loss of two hundred and thirteen, including fifty prisoners. This action is known as the battle of North Point, but has sometimes been called the battle of Long-log Lane.

While Ross's men were approaching Baltimore by land, sixteen vessels of the British fleet moved up the bay, and opened fire upon its immediate defences. The shallowness of the water prevented them from getting near enough to bombard the town itself ; but for twenty-four hours they poured an almost uninterrupted shower of rockets and shells into Fort McHenry, Fort Covington, and the connecting intrenchments. Most of the firing was at long range ; whenever any of the vessels came within reach of the batteries, they were subjected to a fire that quickly drove them back, and in some cases sank them. Fort McHenry, garrisoned by six hundred men under Major George Armistead, bore the brunt of the attack.

At the dead of night the enemy attempted to land a strong force above the forts, for an attack in the rear ; but it was discovered and subjected to a concentrated fire of red-hot shot, which speedily drove it off with serious loss. This practically put an end to the attempt to take Baltimore, and a few hours later the fleet withdrew. The loss of the Americans by the bombardment was four killed and twenty-four wounded. The loss in the fleet is unknown.

This bombardment of Fort McHenry gave us one of our national songs. Francis S. Key had gone out to the British fleet in a row-boat, under a flag of truce, to ask for the release on parole of a friend who had been made prisoner. Admiral Cockburn, who had just completed his plans for the attack, detained him, and in his little boat, moored to the side of the flag-ship, he sat and watched the bombardment. When the second morning broke, and he saw that the flag of the fort — which Cockburn had boasted would "yield in a few hours" — was still flying, he took an old letter out of his pocket, and on the back of it wrote the first draft of "The Star-Spangled Banner." The flag is now in the possession of the Massachusetts Historical Society.

CHAPTER XVIII.

NAVAL BATTLES OF 1814.

Porter's Cruise in the *Essex*—His Campaign Against the Typees—Destruction of the British Whaling Interest in the Pacific—Battle with the *Phœbe* and the *Cherub*—The *Peacock* and the *Epervier*—The *Wasp* and the *Reindeer*—The *Wasp* and the *Avon*—Destruction of the *General Armstrong*—Loss of the *President*—The *Constitution* Captures the *Cyane* and the *Levant*—The *Hornet* and the *Penguin*.

THE naval contests of 1814 and the winter of 1815 repeated and emphasized the lesson of the first year of the war ; they were all, with but two exceptions, American victories.

The remarkable cruise of the *Essex*, commanded by Captain David Porter, begun late in 1812, extended along the coast of South America, around Cape Horn, and throughout almost the entire eastern half of the Pacific, ending in a bloody battle in the harbor of Valparaiso, in March, 1814. The prizes taken in the Atlantic were of little value, except one. The packet ship *Nocton*, captured just south of the equator, had $55,000 in specie on board, with which Porter subsequently paid off his men. She was put in charge of a prize crew, and sailed for the United States, but was recaptured on the way by a British frigate.

Porter had sailed under orders to meet Commodore Bainbridge, who had gone to sea with the *Constitution* and the *Hornet*. But after failing to find either of those vessels at three successive rendezvous, he determined to carry out a plan which he had submitted to the Secretary of the Navy some time before, for a cruise against the British whalers in the Pacific. After the usual stormy passage, he doubled Cape Horn in February, 1813. His description of one of the gales shows us that the greatest dangers undergone by a man-of-war are not always from the guns of the enemy.

"It was with no little joy we now saw ourselves fairly in the Pacific Ocean, calculating on a speedy end to all our sufferings. We began also to form our projects for annoying the enemy, and had already equipped, in imagination, one of their vessels of fourteen or sixteen guns, and manned her from the *Essex*, to cruise against their commerce. Indeed, various were the schemes we formed at this time, and had in fancy immense wealth to return with to our country. But the wind freshened up to a gale, and by noon had reduced us to our storm stay-sail and close-reefed main-top-sail. In the afternoon it hauled around to the westward, and blew with a fury far exceeding anything we had yet experienced, bringing with it such a tremendous sea as to threaten us every moment with destruction, and appalled the stoutest heart on board. Our sails, our standing and running rigging, from the succession of bad weather, had become so damaged as to be no longer trustworthy ; we took, however, the best means in our power to render everything secure, and carried as heavy a press of sail as the ship would bear, to keep her from drifting on the coast of Patagonia, which we had reason to believe was not far distant.

" From the excessive violence with which the wind blew, we had strong hopes that it would be of short continuance ; until, worn out with fatigue and anxiety, greatly alarmed with the terrors of a lee shore, and in momentary expectation of the loss of our masts and bowsprit, we almost considered our situation hopeless. To add to our distress, our pumps had become choked by the shingle ballast, which, from the violent rolling of the ship, had got into them, and the sea had increased to such a height as to threaten to swallow us at every instant. The whole ocean was one continual foam of breakers, and the heaviest squall that I ever experienced had not equalled in violence the most moderate intervals of this tremendous hurricane. We had, however, done all that lay in our power to preserve the ship, and turned our attention to our pumps, which we were enabled to clear, and to keep the ship from drifting on shore, by getting on the most advantageous tack. We were enabled to wear but once ; for the violence of the wind and sea was such as afterward to render it impossible to attempt it, without hazarding the destruction of the ship and the loss of every life on board. Our fatigue had been constant and excessive ; many had been severely bruised by being thrown, by the violent jerks of the ship, down the hatchways, and I was particularly unfortunate in receiving three severe falls, which at length disabled me from going on deck.

" We had shipped several heavy seas, that would have proved destructive to almost any other ship. About three o'clock of the morning of the 3d, the watch only being on deck, an enormous sea broke over the ship, and for an instant destroyed every hope. Our gun-deck ports were burst in, both boats on the quarter stove, our spare spars washed from the chains, our head-rails washed away, and hammock stanchions burst in, and the ship perfectly deluged and water-logged. Immediately after this tremendous shock, which threw the crew into consternation, the gale began to abate, and in the morning we were enabled to set our reefed foresail.

In the height of the gale, Lewis Price, a marine, who had long been confined with a pulmonary complaint, departed this life, and was in the morning committed to the deep ; but the violence of the sea was such that the crew could not be permitted to come on deck to attend the ceremony of his burial, as their weight would have strained and endangered the safety of the ship.

"When this last sea broke on board us, one of the prisoners exclaimed that the ship's broadside was stove in, and that she was sinking. This alarm was greatly calculated to increase the fears of those below, who, from the immense torrent of water that was rushing down the hatchways, had reason to believe the truth of his assertion. Many who were washed from the spar- to the gun-deck, and from their hammocks, and did not know the extent of the injury, were also greatly alarmed ; but the men at the wheel, and some others, who were enabled by a good grasp to keep their stations, distinguished themselves by their coolness and activity after the shock."

Porter touched at the island of Mocha, and afterward ran into the harbor of Valparaiso, where he learned that his arrival in the Pacific was most opportune ; for there were many American whalers that had left home before the war began, and knew

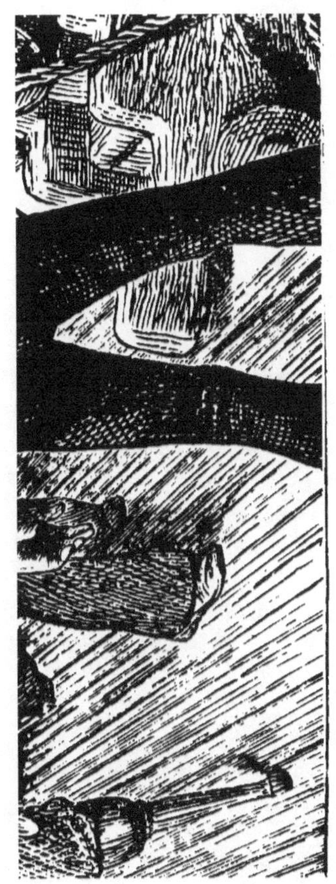

COMMODORE PORTER IN THE PACIFIC OCEAN.

nothing of it, while some English whalers, sailing later, had taken out letters of marque, and carried guns, and were making prizes of the unsuspecting Americans.

Porter soon captured a Peruvian privateer, and two English whalers, and recaptured an American ship that had been taken by the enemy. One of the whalers carried six guns, and the other ten. He placed the entire armament in the faster sailer, cut away her try-works, and with some other alterations converted her into a war-vessel, giving the command of her to John Downes, his first lieutenant. Subsequently a still better ship for the purpose was captured, and the armament was shifted to that, which was then re-christened *Essex Junior*.

With these two ships Porter scoured the ocean for the next six months, and took numerous prizes, nearly all English whalers, several of which had armed themselves as privateers. One he loaded with oil and sent home. Two or three, as he could spare no more men for prize crews, he disarmed and allowed to go home in charge of their own crews, carrying also the other prisoners, all of whom were paroled. One captain, whom he found cruising as a privateer without a commission as such, he put in irons, to be tried as a pirate when the *Essex* should return home. In that six months, Porter and

Downes had captured four thousand tons of British shipping, taking four hundred prisoners ; and as they could now hear of no more in that part of the Pacific, they went in October to the Marquesas Islands, to refit their vessels and let the crews have a rest and a run on shore.

There in the beautiful harbor of Nukahiva they made repairs and wooded and watered at their leisure. Porter formally took possession of the island in the name of the United States, called it Madison's Island, and the harbor Massachusetts Bay, and built a fort on the shore, in which he mounted four guns. Near the fort he constructed a small village, consisting of six houses, a rope-walk, a bakery, and other buildings, which he named Madisonville. His "Journal" gives an interesting account of their life for four or five weeks among the natives of that romantic and then almost unknown group. One of the most exciting incidents of it was a war between two tribes—the Happahs and the Typees—occupying different parts of the island. All the tribes of the island except the Typees had made a sort of treaty of friendship and alliance with Porter. As he and his men were guests of the Happahs, and the Typees had begun to treat them as enemies, Porter felt obliged to join in the war, when the superiority of the fire-arms over the native weapons ended it in the disastrous defeat of the Typees. But this was not accomplished without severe fighting, in which the Typees exhibited the most determined courage, and a great degree of military skill, making the best of such weapons and advantages as they had. Porter's campaign in the Typee valley is one of the most singular episodes in all the annals of war, and the reader will probably be interested in some passages from his account of it, though it has no necessary connection with the subject to which this volume is devoted.

" We arrived at the Typee landing at sunrise, and were joined by ten war-canoes from the Happahs. The *Essex Junior* soon after arrived and anchored. The tops of all the neighboring mountains were covered with the Taeeh and Happah warriors, armed with their spears, clubs, and slings. The beach was covered with the warriors who came with the canoes, and who joined us from the hills. Our force did not amount to a less number than five thousand men ; but not a Typee or any of their dwellings were to be seen. For the whole length of the beach, extending upward of a quarter of a mile, was a clear level plain which extended back about one hundred yards. A high and almost impenetrable swampy thicket bordered on this plain, and the only trace we could perceive which, we were informed, led to the habitations, was a narrow pathway which winded through the swamp.

"The canoes were all hauled on the beach, the Taeehs on the right, the Happahs on the left, and our four boats in the centre. We only waited for reënforcements from the *Essex Junior*, our interpreter, our ambassadors, and Gattanewa [chief of the Happahs]. I went on board to hasten them on shore, and on my return to the beach I found everyone in arms. The Typees had appeared in the bushes, and had pelted our people with stones while they were quietly eating their breakfast.

"I had a man with me who had intermarried with the Typees, and was privileged to go among them, and I furnished him with a white flag and sent him to tell them I had come to offer peace, but was prepared for war. In a few minutes he came running back, and informed me he had met in the bushes an ambuscade of Typees, who had threatened to put him to death if he again ventured among them. In an instant afterward a shower of stones came from the bushes, and at the same moment one of the Typees darted across the pathway and was shot through the leg, but was carried off by his friends.

"Lieutenant Downes arrived with his men, and I

gave the order to march.   We entered the bushes, and were at every instant assailed by spears and stones, which came from different parts of the enemy in ambuscade.   We could hear the snapping of the slings, the whistling of the stones ; the spears came quivering by us, but we could not perceive from whom they came.   No enemy was to be seen, not a whisper was to be heard among them.

" We had advanced about a mile, and came to a small opening on the bank of a river, from the thicket on the opposite side of which we were assailed with a shower of stones, when Lieutenant Downes received a blow which shattered the bone of his left leg, and he fell.   The allied tribes sat as silent observers of our operations ; the sides of the mountains were still covered with them, and I as well as the Taeehs had no slight grounds to doubt the fidelity of the Happahs.   A defeat would have sealed our destruction.

" The Indians began to leave us, and all depended on our own exertions.   I directed Mr. Shaw with four men to escort Lieutenant Downes to the beach, which reduced the number of my men to twenty-four.   We soon came to a place for fording the river, in the thick bushes of the opposite bank of which the Typees made a bold stand.   We endeavored in vain to clear the bushes with our musketry.

The stones and spears flew with augmented numbers.   I directed a volley to be fired, three cheers to
be given, and to dash across the river.   We soon
gained the opposite bank, and continued our march,
rendered still more difficult by the underwood,
which was here so interlaced as to make it necessary sometimes to crawl on our hands and knees.

" On emerging from the swamp, we perceived a
strong and extensive wall of seven feet in height,
raised on an eminence crossing our road, and flanked
on each side by an impenetrable thicket.   In an instant afterward we were assailed by such a shower
of stones, accompanied by the most horrid yells, as
left no doubt that we had here to encounter their
principal strength.   A tree which afforded shelter
from their stones enabled me, accompanied by
Lieutenant Gamble, to annoy them as they rose
above the wall to throw at us ; but these were the
only muskets that could be employed to advantage.

" Finding we could not dislodge them, I gave
orders for taking the place by storm.   But some of
my men had expended all their cartridges, few had
more than three or four remaining, and our only
safety depended on holding our ground till we could
procure a fresh supply.   I despatched Lieutenant
Gamble and four men to the *Essex Junior*, and from
the time of their departure we were chiefly occupied

in eluding the stones, which came with redoubled
force and numbers.   Three of my men were knocked
down by them.   As a feint, we retreated a few
paces, and in an instant the Indians rushed on us
with hideous yells.   The first and second that advanced were killed at the distance of a few paces,
and those who attempted to carry them off were
wounded.   They abandoned their dead, and precipitately retreated to their fort.   Taking advantage of
the terror they were thrown into, we marched off with
our wounded, returning to the beach much fatigued
and with no contemptible opinion of the enemy.

" The next day I determined to proceed with a
force which I believed they could not resist, and
selected two hundred men from the *Essex*, the *Essex
Junior*, and the prizes.   As some of the boats were
leaky, I determined to go by land, over the mountain ridge.   We had a fine, moonlight night, and I
hoped to be down in the Typee valley long before
daylight.

" Not a whisper was heard from one end of the
line to the other.   Our guides marched in front,
and we followed in silence up and down the steep
sides of rocks and mountains, through rivulets,
thickets, and reed-brakes, and by the sides of preci-
pices which sometimes caused us to shudder.   At
twelve o'clock we could hear the drums beating in

the Typee valley, accompanied by loud singing, and the number of lights in different parts of it induced me to believe they were rejoicing. I inquired the cause, and was informed by the Indians that they were celebrating the victory they had obtained over us, and calling on their gods to give them rain in order that it might render our bouhies [muskets] useless.

" The Indians told us it would be impossible to descend without daylight ; and when it was light enough to see down the valley, we were surprised at the height and steepness. A narrow pathway pointed out the track, but it was soon lost among the cliffs. Before I left the hill, I determined by firing a volley to show the natives that our muskets had not received as much injury as they had expected from the rain. As soon as they heard the report, and discovered our number, which, with the multitude of Indians of both tribes who had now assembled, was very numerous, they shouted, beat their drums, and blew their war-conchs from one end of the valley to the other ; and what with the squealing of the hogs, which they now began to catch, the screaming of the women and children, and the yelling of the men, the din was horrible.

" We descended with great difficulty into the village of the Happahs, where everything bore the appearance of a hostile disposition on their part. I sent for their chief, and required to know if they were hostilely disposed. I told him it was necessary we should have something to eat, and that I expected his people to bring us hogs and fruit, and if they did not do so, I should be under the necessity of sending out parties to shoot the hogs and cut down their fruit-trees, as our people were too fatigued to climb them. I also directed that they should lay by their spears and clubs. No notice being taken of these demands, I caused many of their spears and clubs to be taken from them and broken, and sent parties out to shoot hogs, while others were employed in cutting down cocoanut and banana trees until we had a sufficient supply. The chiefs and people now became intimidated, and brought baked hogs in greater abundance than was required.

" At daylight next morning the line of march was formed. On ascending the ridge where we had passed such a disagreeable night, we halted to take breath, and view for a few minutes the delightful valley which was soon to become a scene of desolation. We had a distant view of every part. The valley was about nine miles in length, and three or four in breadth, surrounded on every part, except the beach, by lofty mountains. The upper part was bounded by a precipice many hundred feet in height, from the top of which a handsome sheet of water was precipitated, and formed a beautiful river which ran meandering through the valley. Villages were scattered here and there ; the bread-fruit and cocoanut trees flourished luxuriantly and in abundance ; plantations laid out in good order, enclosed with stone walls, were in a high state of cultivation ; and everything bespoke industry, abundance, and happiness. Never in my life did I witness a more delightful scene or experience more repugnance than I now felt for the necessity which compelled me to punish a happy and heroic people.

" A large assembly of Typee warriors were posted on the opposite banks of the river, and dared us to descend. In their rear was a fortified village, secured by strong stone walls. Drums were beating and war-conchs sounding, and we soon found they were making every effort to oppose us.

" As soon as we reached the foot of the mountain we were annoyed by a shower of stones from the bushes and from behind stone walls. After resting a few minutes, I directed the scouting parties to gain the opposite bank of the river, and followed with the main body. The fortified village was taken without loss on our side ; but their chief warrior and another were killed, and several wounded. They retreated only to stone walls on higher ground, where they continued to sling their stones and throw their spears.   Three of my men were wounded, and many of the Typees killed, before we dislodged them.

" Parties were sent out to scour the woods, and another fort was taken after some resistance ; but the party, overpowered by numbers, were compelled to retreat to the main body, after keeping possession of it half an hour.   We were waiting, in the fort first taken, for the return of our scouting parties.   A multitude of Tayees and Happahs were with us, and many were on the outskirts of the village, seeking for plunder.   Lieutenant McKnight had driven a party from a strong wall on the high ground, and had possession of it, when a large party of Typees, who had been 'lying in ambush, rushed by his fire and darted into the fort with their spears.   The Tayeehs and Happahs all ran.   The Typees approached within pistol-shot, but on the first fire retreated precipitately, crossing the fire of McKnight's party, and although none fell, we had reason to believe that many were wounded.   The spears and stones were flying from the bushes in every direction ; and although we killed and wounded in this place great numbers of them, we were satisfied that we should have to fight our way through the whole valley.

"I sent a messenger to inform the Typees that we should cease hostilities when they no longer made resistance, but so long as stones were thrown I should destroy their villages. No notice was taken of this message.

"We continued our march up the valley, and met in our way several beautiful villages, which we set on fire, and at length arrived at their capital—for it deserves the name of one. We had been compelled to fight every inch of ground, and here they made considerable opposition. The place was soon carried, however, and I very reluctantly set fire to it. The beauty and regularity of this place were such as to strike every spectator with astonishment. Their public square was far superior to any other we had met with. Numbers of their gods were here destroyed ; several large and elegant new war-canoes were burned in the houses that sheltered them, and many of their drums were thrown into the flames. Our Indians loaded themselves with plunder, after destroying bread-fruit and other trees and all the young plants they could find. We had now arrived at the upper end of the valley, about nine miles from the beach, and at the foot of the waterfall above mentioned.

"After resting about half an hour, I directed the Indians to take care of our wounded, and we formed the line of march and proceeded down the valley, in our route destroying several other villages, at all of which we had some skirmishing. At one of these places, at the foot of a steep hill, the enemy rolled down enormous stones, with a view of crushing us to death. The number of villages destroyed amounted to ten ; and the destruction of trees and plants, and the plunder carried off by the Indians, was almost incredible. The Typees fought us to the last, and even at first harassed our rear on our return ; but parties left in ambush soon put a stop to further annoyance.

" We at length came to the formidable fort which checked our career on our first day's enterprise, and although I had witnessed many instances of the great exertion and ingenuity of these islanders, I never had supposed them capable of contriving and erecting a work like this. It formed the segment of a circle, and was about fifty yards in extent, built of large stones, six feet thick at the bottom and gradually narrowing to the top. On the left was a narrow entrance, merely sufficient to admit one person's entering. The wings and rear were equally guarded, and the right was flanked by another fortification of greater magnitude and equal strength and ingenuity. I directed the Indians and my own men to put their shoulders to the wall and endeavor to throw it down ; but no impression could be made upon it. It appeared of ancient date, and time alone can destroy it. We succeeded in making a small breach, through which we passed on our route to the beach,— a route which was familiar to us, but had now become doubly intricate from the number of trees which had since been cut down and placed across the pathway.

"The chiefs of the Happahs invited me to return to their valley, assuring me that an abundance of everything was already provided for us ; and the girls, who had assembled in great numbers, dressed out in their best attire, welcomed me with smiles. Gattanewa met me on the side of the hill as I was ascending.   The old man's heart was full ; he could not speak ; he placed both my hands on his head, rested his forehead on my knees, and after a short pause, raising himself, placed his hands on my breast, and. exclaimed *Gattanewa !* and then on his own and said *Apotee !* [Porter] to remind me we had exchanged names.

"When I reached the summit of the mountain, I stopped to contemplate that valley which in the morning we had viewed in all its beauty. A long line of smoking ruins now marked our traces from one end to the other, the opposite hills were covered with the unhappy fugitives, and the whole presented a scene of desolation and horror. Unhappy and heroic people ! the victims of your own courage and mistaken pride. While the instruments of your fate shed the tear of pity over your misfortunes, thousands of your countrymen — nay, brethren of the same family — triumphed in your distresses.

" The day of our return was devoted to rest. But a messenger was despatched to the Typees to inform them I was still willing to make peace, and that I should not allow them to return to their valley until they had come on terms of friendship with us, and exchanged presents. They readily consented to the terms, and requested to know the number of hogs I should require. I told them I should expect from them four hundred, which they assured me should be delivered without delay.

" Flags were now sent from all the other tribes, with large presents of hogs and fruit, and peace was established throughout the island. The chiefs, the priests, and the principal persons of the tribes were very solicitous of forming a relationship with me by an exchange of names with some of my family. Some wished to bear the name of my brother, my son-in-law, my brother-in-law, etc., and when all the male stock were exhausted, they as anxiously solicited the names of the other sex. The name of my son, however, was more desired than any other, and many old men, whose long gray beards rendered their appearance venerable, were known by the name of *Pickaneenee Apotee ;* the word ' pickaninny ' having been introduced among them by the sailors.''

Captain Porter was undoubtedly sincere in the belief that what he had done was a necessity of war. But when we consider that it arose simply from the refusal of a people, standing on their own ground, to enter into a treaty of amity with strangers whose language they could not speak, and whose purposes they did not understand, it looks as if the captain had imposed a pretty heavy penalty for a small offence, and given the unfortunate Typees as unfair treatment as he himself experienced a few months later in the harbor of Valparaiso.

Meanwhile, Captain Porter had learned that an English frigate had been sent out to stop his career ; and as whalers had now become scarce, and he had taken as many prizes as he could well manage, after refitting at the Marquesas Islands, he sailed in search of his enemy. The truth was, Captain James Hillyar, of the British navy, was looking for him with *two* ships, the *Phœbe* and the *Cherub*, mounting respectively fifty-three and twenty-eight guns ; and there is good reason to believe that the Admiralty had sent him out with stringent orders to find and destroy or capture the *Essex* at all hazards. He found her at Valparaiso, and blockaded her there for six weeks. On one occasion the *Essex* and the *Phœbe* almost fouled, through the fault of the latter, and Porter called away his boarders and in a moment more would have been on the Englishman's deck ; but Hillyar protested so earnestly that he had no intention of attacking in a neutral port, that he was permitted to withdraw from his suspicious position. Had Porter been more shrewd and less chivalrous, he would perhaps have seen that there was no way to account for the position of the *Phœbe*, except on the supposition that Hillyar was intending to carry the *Essex* by boarding, had he not found her commander and crew too ready for him. That he cared nothing for the neutrality of the port, was demonstrated by his subsequent conduct.

After vainly offering battle on equal terms, Porter, on the 28th of March, attempted to put to sea. But his ship was struck by a heavy squall, which carried away the main-top-mast. Being pursued by the *Phœbe* and *Cherub*, he tacked about, reëntered the harbor, and anchored within pistol-shot of the shore. Paying not the slightest regard to the neutrality of the port, the enemy followed the *Essex*, took a position under her stern, and opened fire. Even under this disadvantage, Porter got three long guns out at the stern ports, and fought them so skilfully that in half an hour both the *Phœbe* and the *Cherub* drew off for repairs. They next took a position on the starboard quarter, out of reach of the carronades that composed the *Essex's* broadside, and fired at her with their long guns. Under his flying jib, the only sail he could set, Porter ran down upon the enemy, and after a short and intense action at close range, drove off the *Cherub*. But the *Phœbe* edged away again out of reach of his carronades, and kept up a steady fire from her long guns. The slaughter on board the *Essex* was sickening. At one gun, three whole crews were swept away in succession. Says Captain Porter, in his " Journal :" " I was informed that the cockpit, the steerage, the ward-room, and the berth-deck could contain no more wounded ; that the wounded were killed while the surgeons were dressing them ; and that, unless something was speedily done to prevent it, the ship would soon sink from the number of shot-holes in her bottom."

The captain next tried to run her ashore ; but while she was still nearly a mile from the land, the wind suddenly shifted. A hawser was bent to the sheet anchor, and the ship swung round so as to bring her broadside to bear on the enemy, but the hawser soon parted. Indeed, she had anchored in the first place with springs on her cables, but the springs had been repeatedly shot away.*

With all these misfortunes, the ship took fire, and as the flames burst up the hatchways Porter ordered all who could swim to jump overboard and strike out for the shore, as the boats had been destroyed by the enemy's shot. The flames were extinguished ; but the *Essex* was now a wreck, deliberately raked by every discharge from her antagonist, and the colors were struck. The *Essex Junior* had been in no condition to assist in the fight, but was included in the surrender. Out of two hundred and fifty-five men, Porter had lost one hundred and fifty-four in killed, wounded, or missing. Hillyar reported the loss on his two ships as five killed and ten wounded.

The battle had been witnessed by thousands of people on shore. So near were the vessels to land a part of the time, that many of the *Phœbe's* shot struck the beach. The United States Consul, Joel R. Poinsett, protested to the Chilian authorities

---

* A " spring " of this sort is a rope, one end of which is attached to the cable and the other end carried to the after part of the ship, so that by hauling upon it she can be swung round to point her broadside in any desired direction. A high authority — Farragut — says one of Porter's serious mistakes in this action was in fastening the springs to the cable, when they should have been fastened to the anchor, which would have carried the greater part of them below the surface of the water, out of the reach of shot.

against the violation of neutrality, and demanded that the batteries protect the *Essex ;* but he received no satisfactory answer, and took the first opportunity of leaving the country. Captain Porter estimated that it had cost the British Government nearly six million dollars to possess his ship.

Among the crew of the *Essex* was a midshipman twelve years old, who subsequently became the greatest of all naval commanders, David G. Farragut. In his " Journal " he describes vividly the battle and the part he took in it. Some passages will be of interest here, as they present pictures seldom found in the descriptions of such contests :

" I well remember the feelings of awe produced in me by the approach of the hostile ships ; even to my young mind it was perceptible in the faces of those around me, as clearly as possible, that our case was hopeless. It was equally apparent that all were ready to die at their guns, rather than surrender ; and such I believe to have been the determination of the crew, almost to a man. There had been so much bantering of each other between the men of the ships, through the medium of letters and songs, with an invariable fight between the boats' crews when they met on shore, that a very hostile sentiment was engendered. Our flags were flying from every mast, and the enemy's vessels displayed their ensigns, jacks, and motto-flags, as they bore down grandly to the attack.

" I performed the duties of captain's aid, quarter-gunner, powder-boy, and in fact did everything that was required of me. I shall never forget the horrid impression made upon me by the sight of the first man I had ever seen killed. He was a boatswain's mate, and was fearfully mutilated. It staggered and sickened me at first ; but they soon began to fall around me so fast that it all appeared like a dream, and produced no effect on my nerves. I can remember well, while I was standing near the captain, just abaft the mainmast, a shot came through the water-ways and glanced upward, killing four men who were standing by the side of the gun, taking the last one in the head and scattering his brains over both of us. But this awful sight did not affect me half as much as the death of the first poor fellow. I neither thought of nor noticed anything but the working of the guns.

" On one occasion Midshipman Isaacs came up to the captain and reported that a quarter-gunner named Roach had deserted his post. The only reply of the captain, addressed to me, was, ' Do your duty, sir.' I seized a pistol and went in pursuit of the fellow, but did not find him.

" Soon after this, some gun-primers were wanted,

and I was sent after them. In going below, while
I was on the ward-room ladder, the captain of the
gun directly opposite the hatchway was struck full
in the face by an eighteen-pound shot, and fell back
on me. We tumbled down the hatch together. I
struck on my head, and fortunately he fell on my
hips. As he was a man of at least two hundred
pounds' weight, I would have been crushed to death
if he had fallen directly across my body. I lay for
some moments stunned by the blow, but soon recovered consciousness enough to rush up on deck. The
captain, seeing me covered with blood, asked if I
was wounded, to which I replied, ' I believe not,
sir.' ' Then,' said he, ' where are the primers ? '
This first brought me completely to my senses, and
I ran below again and carried the primers on deck.
When I came up the second time, I saw the captain
fall, and in my turn ran up and asked if he was
wounded. He answered me almost in the same
words, ' I believe not, my son ; but I felt a blow on
the top of my head.' He must have been knocked
down by the windage of a passing shot.

" When my services were not required for other
purposes, I generally assisted in working a gun ;
would run and bring powder from the boys, and
send them back for more, until the captain wanted
me to carry a message.

" I have already remarked how soon I became accustomed to scenes of blood and death during the action ; but after the battle had ceased, when, on going below, I saw the mangled bodies of my shipmates, dead and dying, groaning and expiring with the most patriotic sentiments on their lips, I became faint and sick. As soon as I recovered from the first shock, however, I hastened to assist the surgeon. Among the badly wounded was one of my best friends, Lieutenant J. G. Cowell. When I spoke to him he said, ' O Davy, I fear it is all up with me.' I found that he had lost a leg just above the knee, and the doctor informed me that his life might have been saved if he had consented to the amputation of the limb an hour before ; but when it was proposed to drop another patient and attend to him, he replied, ' No, doctor, none of that ; fair play is a jewel. One man's life is as dear as another's ; I would not cheat any poor fellow out of his turn.' Thus died one of the best officers and bravest men among us.

" It was wonderful to find dying men, who had hardly ever attracted notice among the ship's company, uttering sentiments worthy of a Washington. You might have heard in all directions, ' Don't give her up, Logan ! ' — a sobriquet for Porter — ' Hurrah for liberty ! ' and similar expressions. A young

Scotchman named Bissley had one leg shot off close to the groin. He used his handkerchief for a tourniquet, and said to his comrades, ' I left my own country and adopted the United States, to fight for her. I hope I have this day proved myself worthy of the country of my adoption. I am no longer of any use to you or to her, so good-by ! ' With these words, he leaned on the sill of the port and threw himself overboard.

" Lieutenant Wilmer, who had been sent forward to let go the sheet anchor, was knocked overboard by a shot. After the action, his little Negro boy, Ruff, came on deck and asked me what had become of his master, and when I imparted to him the sad news, he deliberately jumped into the sea and was drowned.

" I went on board the *Phœbe* about 8 A.M. on the 29th, and was ushered into the steerage. I was so mortified at our capture that I could not refrain from tears. While in this uncomfortable state, I was aroused by hearing a young reefer call out, ' A prize ! a prize ! Ho, boys, a fine grunter, by Jove ! ' I saw at once that he had under his arm a pet pig belonging to our ship, called Murphy. I claimed the animal as my own. ' Ah,' said he, ' but you are a prisoner, and your pig also.' ' We always respect private property,' I replied, and as I had seized hold of Murphy I determined not to let go, unless compelled by superior force. This was fun for the oldsters, who immediately sung out, ' Go it, my little Yankee ! If you can thrash Shorty, you shall have your pig ! ' ' Agreed ! ' said I. A ring was formed, and at it we went. I soon found that my antagonist's pugilistic education did not come up to mine. In fact, he was no match for me, and was compelled to give up the pig. So I took Master Murphy under my arm, feeling that I had in some degree wiped out the disgrace of our defeat.''

Porter and his surviving men were paroled, and the *Essex Junior* was converted into a cartel, in which they were sent home to New York. When she was within about thirty miles of her destination, she was overhauled by a British war-vessel and detained all night, which by the terms of the agreement with Captain Hillyar absolved them from their parole. In the morning Captain Porter with a few men left the ship in a small boat, unnoticed, and pulled for shore, landing at Babylon, Long Island, about sunset. He was immediately made a prisoner by the militia ; but when he exhibited his commission, they fired a salute of twenty-one guns and furnished a horse and cart to carry his boat. On reaching New York, he received a grand ovation, and as he rode through the streets the people unhitched his horses and drew the carriage themselves.   Thus ended one of the most exciting, varied, and romantic cruises ever made by a modern sailor.

On the 29th of April the American sloop-of-war *Peacock*, carrying eighteen guns and commanded by Captain Lewis Warrington, was cruising off the coast of Florida when she sighted the British brig-of-war *Epervier*, eighteen guns, convoying three merchantmen.   The two men-of-war hauled up for action, and after a battle of forty-two minutes the English flag was struck.   The *Epervier* had lost twenty-two men killed or wounded, her rigging was badly cut up, and there was five feet of water in the hold, more than forty shot having entered her hull. The *Peacock*, which was much heavier than her antagonist, had received very little injury, and but two of her crew were wounded.   The prize had $118,000 in specie on board.   Soon after this the *Peacock* cruised in the Bay of Biscay and along the coast of Portugal, and captured fourteen merchantmen.

Captain Johnston Blakeley, in the *Wasp*, a sister ship to the *Peacock*, sailed from Portsmouth, N. H., for a cruise in the chops of the English Channel. At daylight on the 28th of June he sighted two sail on the lee beam and one on the weather beam. Avoiding the former, he made for the latter, which proved to be the British brig *Reindeer*, of eighteen guns. There was considerable manœuvring for the weather-gauge, but the Englishman succeeded in keeping it, and by three o'clock had come within sixty yards. At that short distance she had five shots at the *Wasp*, with a shifting carronade, firing round shot and grape, before the *Wasp* could bring a single gun to bear on her. But Blakeley then made. a half-board, and by firing from aft forward finally brought every gun into use. This was too heavy for the *Reindeer*, and she ran into the *Wasp* and attempted to board, her crew being led by Captain Manners in person. But every attempt was repelled by the crew of the *Wasp*, and when Captain Blakeley ordered them in turn to board the enemy, they were on her deck and the British flag was hauled down in one minute. The whole action had lasted but half an hour. The *Reindeer* had lost twenty-five killed, including her captain, and forty-two wounded ; the *Wasp*, five killed and twenty-two wounded. The upper half of the hull of the *Reindeer* was a complete wreck, and she had to be burned. A few weeks later, September 1st, the *Wasp*, after making three prizes, discovered four sail and bore up for the most weatherly of them. Between nine and ten o'clock at night the two ships came close together, and broadsides were exchanged till the enemy became silent. Blakeley hailed, and

was answered that she surrendered. She was the
British brig *Avon*, of eighteen guns. But before
the Americans had taken possession of her, another
British man-of-war came up. The *Wasp* made ready
to engage her ; but before she could do so, two others appeared, and she then put up her helm and ran
off before the wind. It was afterward learned that
the *Avon* had sunk, and her consort with difficulty
rescued the survivors of her crew. In the next twenty
days the *Wasp* took three prizes, and then, continu-
ing her cruise, was never heard from again.

One of the bloodiest sea-fights of this year took
place in the harbor of Fayal, Azores. The American privateer *General Armstrong*, carrying fourteen
guns and ninety men, commanded by Captain Samuel C. Reid, put in there for water on the 26th of
September. A few hours later, three British war-
vessels — the *Plantagenet*, *Carnation*, and *Rota* —
entered the harbor. It was a neutral port, but they
cared no more for its neutrality than Hillyar had
cared for that of Valparaiso.

In the evening, under a full moon, four armed
boats were sent from these vessels to cut out the
privateer. As they approached her, they were
warned off several times, but paid no attention to it,
and attempted to board. Reid then opened fire on
them, and drove them off with heavy loss. For

greater security, the *Armstrong* was hauled up close to the fort, and moored. The Governor remonstrated with Captain Van Lloyd, commander of the English fleet ; to which the captain answered that he was determined to destroy the privateer, and if the fort protected her he would bombard the town till not a house was left standing.

At midnight the *Armstrong* was attacked again, this time by fourteen launches, each carrying about fifty men. Reid promptly opened his broadside on them, with terrible effect ; yet two or three of them succeeded in reaching the vessel, and the crew then met them with cutlass and pistol, and scarcely a man in them was left alive. A letter written from Fayal at the time, by an Englishman, says the officers in charge of the boats cheered on their men with a shout of " No quarter !" and that " the Americans fought with great firmness, but more like bloodthirsty savages than anything else. They rushed into the boats, sword in hand, and put every soul to death, as far as came within their power. Several boats floated on shore, full of dead bodies."

Next morning, the *Carnation* sailed in and engaged the *Armstrong;* but after a short action she was badly cut up and obliged to haul off for repairs. Several guns on the *Armstrong* had been dismounted ; and as Captain Reid now saw that her ultimate destruction was certain, he cut away her masts, blew a hole in her bottom, and went ashore with his men. Two of the crew had been killed, and seven wounded. The ascertained loss of the British was one hundred and twenty killed and ninety wounded.

After burning the abandoned wreck, Van Lloyd demanded of the Governor that the gallant little crew he had failed to capture should be given up to him as prisoners. This modest request was of course refused, and Captain Reid and his men then took possession of an old convent, declaring that they would defend themselves to the last. But they were not molested.

The vessel that was despatched to England to take home the British sailors wounded in this action, was not permitted to carry a single letter from anybody. Indeed, not only this affair, says Cobbett in his " Letters," but the loss of the *Avon*, the battle of Plattsburg, and other actions not creditable to the English arms, were carefully concealed from the English public. At the demand of Portugal, the British Government apologized for the violation of neutrality ; but the owners of the *Armstrong* never obtained any indemnity.

This was the last naval action before the declaration of peace ; but as that declaration did not immediately reach the cruisers at sea, three others were fought. On the 15th of January, 1815, Commodore Decatur, in the *President*, had a prolonged battle with the frigate *Endymion*, off Long Island, and reduced her to a wreck. But two other British cruisers came up, and he was compelled to surrender. He had lost eighty men killed or wounded. On the 20th of February, the *Constitution*, Captain Charles Stewart, off the coast of Portugal, captured both the *Cyane*, of thirty-four guns, and the *Levant*, of twenty-one, after a battle of forty minutes, in which he lost fifteen men, and inflicted a loss of about forty. The *Levant* was subsequently recaptured by three English cruisers, while she was in Port Praya, another neutral harbor. On the 23d of March, the American brig *Hornet*, Captain James Biddle, and the British brig *Penguin*, Captain Dickenson, being almost exactly matched in men and metal, fought a battle of twenty-two minutes' duration, off the island of Tristan d'Acunha, at the close of which the *Penguin*, having lost forty-two men and been badly crippled, surrendered. Her commander was killed. The *Hornet* had one man killed and ten wounded. This was the last of what the London *Times* had fallen into the habit of calling " the painful events at sea."

CHAPTER XIX.

THE HARTFORD CONVENTION.

Attitude of the Federalists, Real and Imputed—The Convention at Hartford—Its Popular Reputation—What General Scott did not say at Chippewa.

WHEN a destructive war had been carried on for two years, when recruiting was slow, and the Government heavily in debt, and yet no way appeared but to fight it out, it might have been expected that harsh criticism of the policy of the Administration, coming from the party that had steadily opposed the war, would subject that party to the charge of being unpatriotic and untrue to the Union. It might also have been expected that an opposition which had become chronic could not but become in some respects unjust. So when the Federalists in 1814 were flooding the Legislatures of New England with memorials on the conduct of the war, they could hardly restrain themselves from overdrawing the picture of its failures, or from representing the condition of things before the war as rather more paradisiacal than anybody had suspected. And on the other hand, they were accused not only of rejoicing in defeats of the national arms, but of plotting a separation of New England from the other States, with a view of ultimately making her again a part of the British Empire. That there were some Federalists who contemplated a dissolution of the Union as a possible remedy for certain difficulties, is quite probable, for such views were at that time not confined to either party. The contingency of disunion was frequently discussed by men of both parties. But that anybody seriously contemplated a reunion with England, there has never been any evidence worth considering. The story was gotten up by the Administration party, in order to cast odium upon the Federalists ; and the occurrence most freely used to give color to it was the Hartford Convention, which unfortunately sat with closed doors, and thus was easily misrepresented as a treasonable gathering.

In the third year of the war the hand of the enemy had fallen heavily upon the coast of New England, and at the same time an unpleasant feeling had arisen from the refusal of the United States Government to pay the militia that had been in service under State officers. In this crisis, the Legislature of Massachusetts, on the 16th of October, by a vote of 260 to 90, passed a series of resolutions, the fifth of which authorized the calling of a convention to confer "upon the subject of their [the New England States] public grievances and concerns ; and upon the best means of preserving our resources ; and of defence against the enemy ; and to devise and suggest for adoption by those respective States such measures as they may deem expedient ; and also to take measures, if they shall think it proper, for procuring a convention of delegates from all the United States, in order to revise the Constitution thereof, and more effectually to secure the support and attachment of all the people, by placing all upon the basis of fair representation." The letter addressed to the governors of other States set forth the general objects of the proposed conference to be, " to deliberate upon the dangers to which the eastern section of the Union is exposed by the course of the war, and to devise, if practicable, means of security and defence which may be consistent with the preservation of their resources from total ruin, and adapted to their local situation, mutual relations, and habits, and not repugnant to their obligations as members of the Union."

In response to this call, a convention of twenty-six delegates met at Hartford, Conn., December 15th, and sat for three weeks. All sorts of absurd rumors as to the purpose of the Convention were set afloat, and the President so far participated in the vague fears thus excited, or pretended to, as to station a regiment of troops in Hartford.

On the 5th of January, 1815, the Convention adjourned, and published a long report, wherein were set forth the difficulties that the country labored under, and methods proposed by the Convention for adjusting them. These were first discussed at length, and then summarized in a series of resolutions : That unconstitutional drafts of militia should be prevented ; that the New England States should be empowered to defend their own territory against the enemy ; that representatives and direct taxes should be apportioned among the States according to the number of their free inhabitants ; that a two-third vote of Congress should be required to admit a new State ; that embargoes for more than sixty days should be forbidden ; that a two-third Congressional vote should be required for the interdiction of commercial intercourse, or for the declaration of offensive war ; that naturalized citizens should not be eligible to Federal offices ; that the President should be ineligible for a second term, and should not be chosen from the same State twice in succession ; and, finally, that if these ends were not attained, and peace not concluded, another convention should be held in Boston in the following June.

This ought to have been plain enough for anybody to understand ; and yet allusions to " the old blue-lights of the Hartford Convention," as a synonym for treason, have come down to our own day. Its popularity as a bugbear has never been exceeded. So great was its influence in this regard, that it caused General Scott to remember something which had never taken place.   In his account of the battle of Chippewa he says : " And now the New England States were preparing to hold a convention — it met at Hartford — perhaps to secede from the Union — possibly to take up arms against it.   Scott's brigade, nearly all New England men, were most indignant, and this was the subject of the second of the three pithy remarks made to them by Scott just before the final conflict of Chippewa.   Calling aloud to the gallant Major Hindman, he said, ' Let us put down the Federal Convention by beating the enemy in front.   There's nothing in the Constitution against that.' " *   There can be no question as to the intrinsic pithiness of this remark ; but if Scott made it, he must have been somewhat of a prophet, for the battle of Chippewa was fought on the 5th of July, and the call for the Convention was not issued till October.   This shows the danger of writing

---

* Scott's Memoirs, vol. i., page 133.

memoirs half a century after the events of which they treat.

The great news from the South, and the tidings of peace, followed so quickly upon the adjournment of the Convention that its labors went for nought, its members were subjected to merciless ridicule, and the new convention proposed for June was never held.

CHAPTER XX.

THE CAMPAIGN ON THE GULF COAST.

British Occupation of Pensacola—Negotiations with Lafitte—Expedition against Mobile—Capture of Pensacola—Defence of New Orleans—The Battles before the City—Defeat of the British—Losses.

THOUGH Pensacola was a Spanish town, in Spanish territory, the British forces used it as a station for fitting out expeditions against Mobile and New Orleans. Here they gathered arms and munitions of war ; here their vessels found safe anchorage in a spacious harbor, where they were afforded every facility for refitting ; and here the savage allies were equipped for war and murder. The British commander sent an embassy to Jean Lafitte, at Barataria Bay, offering him a captain's commission, together with a free pardon for all his gang, and grants of land to be carved out of such territory as might be conquered from the United States, on condition that he and his men would assist with their fleet the expeditions then fitting out. The English commander also hinted darkly at something which he called " the blessings of the British constitution"—probably meaning the abundant bone and muscle of a beef-eater—as an additional inducement to the famous little Frenchman.   Lafitte was commonly called a pirate, but that was not precisely his character.   He was a receiver of stolen goods captured by half piratical privateers, which he smuggled into New Orleans.   But, pirate or no pirate, he seems to have been too shrewd for the Englishman.   He appeared to acquiesce till he obtained the terms in black and white, and then despatched the letters to Governor Claiborne of Louisiana, together with one in which he offered his services in defending the coast against the British, on condition that the proscription of himself and his adherents be terminated by an act of oblivion.   The Governor laid the letters before a council of military and naval officers, who decided that they were forgeries and Lafitte a scoundrel.   Consequently an expedition under Commodore Patterson was sent against him, by which his establishment was broken up, nine of his vessels were seized, and many of his men made prisoners.

One morning in July, General Jackson was presented with a new English musket, brought to his headquarters by a friendly Indian who had received it from the Creeks at Appalachicola.   This told an alarming story, which the General at once communicated to Governor Claiborne and the Secretary of War.   Of the latter he asked permission to make a descent upon Pensacola. Before an answer was received, Jackson was joined by new levies of troops from Tennessee, which he hurried to Mobile.

On Mobile Point, commanding the entrance to the bay, stood a ruinous earthwork known as Fort Bowyer. Major William Lawrence, with a garrison of one hundred and sixty men, took possession of this, and proceeded to put it in shape for defence. On the 12th of September, the British landed a detachment of marines and six hundred Indians on the peninsula of which Mobile Point is the extremity, and a few hours later four war-vessels, under Captain Percy, appeared at the entrance of the bay. Two or three days were passed in feeble demonstrations on the land side, and attempts to sound the channel; but on the afternoon of the 15th the fleet sailed up in line, dropped anchor in the channel, and opened the battle. For an hour the firing was incessant; it ceased for a moment when the colors of the flag-ship *Hermes* were shot away; but was soon renewed, when a chance shot cut the cable of the *Hermes*, the current swung her bow-on to the fort, and for twenty minutes she was raked mercilessly. She drifted down the channel and ran aground, when Captain Percy abandoned her and set her on fire. Another vessel was crippled and driven off, and the other two then withdrew.

The simultaneous assaults of the marines and Indians had been met and repelled with a few discharges of grape. In this action the garrison lost four men killed and four wounded ; the British official report acknowledged a loss of thirty-two killed and forty wounded.

Early in November, Jackson, with three thousand men, marched on Pensacola, where he proposed to garrison the forts till the Spanish authorities were able to maintain for themselves the neutrality of the port. This proposition being rejected by the Spanish Governor, Jackson's men charged into the town and captured a battery, and took possession. That night Fort Barrancas, commanding the entrance to the harbor, was blown up, and the British vessels sailed away.

Hurrying back to Mobile, where he feared a second attack, Jackson learned of the revelations of Lafitte and was urged to go to the defence of New Orleans. He arrived in that city on the 2d of December, was enthusiastically welcomed, and at once set to work to prepare it for defence. He called out the Louisiana militia, appealed to the free negroes, released and enrolled convicts whose terms were within two months of expiration, accepted the services of Lafitte and his men, assigning them to duty as artillerists, and ordered Coffee with his two thousand men to join him from Mobile. While looking anxiously for new levies from Kentucky and Tennessee, who were to come by way of the river, he fortified the city, and proclaimed martial law.

On the 10th of December the British fleet entered Lake Borgne, where on the 14th it defeated and captured the American gunboats. On the 23d a body of two thousand four hundred British troops reached the bank of the Mississippi nine miles below New Orleans, and with two thousand one hundred Jackson went down to meet them.

New Orleans was the largest prize which had been contended for in this war. It was a city of twenty thousand inhabitants ; and a hundred and fifty thousand bales of cotton, worth two shillings a pound, were stored there. But it was not so much its immediate pecuniary value that tempted the enemy, as the commercial and strategical importance of its position, for they expected not only to capt-ure but to hold it permanently. Lieutenant Gleig, author of " The Subaltern," who was connected with the expedition, after describing the Mississippi and its tributaries, wrote : " Whatever nation, therefore, chances to possess this place, possesses in reality the command of a greater extent of country than is included within the boundary line of the whole United States," and the London *Times*, announcing that all the disposable shipping had been sent from Bermuda to the Mississippi, added that, "most active measures are pursuing for detaching from the dominion of the enemy an important part of his territory."

Wellington's veterans, fresh from their victories in the Spanish peninsula, were now before the city, and the inhabitants, knowing how hasty had been the preparations for defence, trembled for its safety. The expectation was, that, if captured, it would at once be sacked.

It was late in the day when Jackson moved to the attack. He sent Coffee and his Tennesseeans to gain the right flank and rear of the enemy, while the rest of his forces were to deploy across the narrow strip of land between the river and a morass, and attack in front. The schooner *Carolina* was ordered to move down to a point opposite the British left, and enfilade the position ; her first discharge to be the signal for the land attack. It was half-past seven o'clock when she opened the battle with a broadside that tore through the British camp and swept down a large number of men. The moon was young and obscured by clouds, so that there was almost absolute darkness, except when the flashes of the guns momentarily lighted up one or another part of the field.

The two armies soon became intermingled, and, as one of the participants wrote, " no man could tell what was going forward in any quarter, except where he himself chanced immediately to stand ; no one part of the line could bring assistance to another, because in truth no line existed." The fighting was mostly hand-to-hand ; few of the Americans had bayonets, but many carried long knives, and the most ghastly wounds were given and received. Officers on either side would gather little companies of men and go out into the darkness to find the enemy ; but when they had come in contact with an armed party like themselves, it was often impossible to say whether they were friends or foes.

After three hours of this bloody work, the Americans withdrew to works four miles from the city. They had lost twenty-four killed, one hundred and fifteen wounded, and seventy-four missing. General Keane's official report made the British loss forty-six killed, one hundred and sixty-seven wounded, and sixty-four missing. Lieutenant Gleig, in his " Narrative," says, " Not less than five hundred men had fallen, many of whom were our finest soldiers and best officers ; and yet we could not but consider ourselves fortunate in escaping from the toils, even at the expense of so great a sacrifice." A journal found upon a British officer who was killed in the battle of January 8th, puts the loss in this action at "two hundred and twenty-four killed, and an immense number wounded."

Heavy reënforcements of British troops soon arrived, and with them Generals Sir Edward Pakenham and Samuel Gibbs. Pakenham, a brother-in-law of the Duke of Wellington, had won considerable distinction in the Peninsular War. He found the army before New Orleans in a pitiful plight. It was encamped on a strip of low and level land, on one side a broad river where it had no vessels, and on the other an almost impassable morass. In front were fortifications that were continually being strengthened, and of the enemy behind them almost nothing was known ; while two armed vessels kept up day and night an enfilading fire. With all this, alternate rain and frost left them scarcely a comfortable hour.

Pakenham's first movement was to bring heavy guns and a furnace across the peninsula by night, and plant them on the levee ; from which on the morning of the 27th he opened a fire with hot shot, and in half an hour had driven the *Louisiana* up stream and set the *Carolina* on fire, so that she was abandoned and blew up.

On the 28th he made a reconnoissance in force. As the left wing approached the American lines, a group of buildings which Jackson's men had filled with combustibles was fired by a hot shot from one of his guns, and amid the heat and smoke the British saw before them an impassable ditch, from behind which a few pieces of artillery, handled with the utmost skill, poured destruction through their ranks. The right wing found the left of Jackson's position weak, effected a lodgment within the lines, and might perhaps have changed the fortunes of the campaign, had not its leader been instructed that this was to be a reconnoissance, not a battle.

Pakenham now resolved upon regular siege operations, and brought thirty guns from the fleet, which in the night of the 31st he mounted within three hundred yards of the American lines. His troops were encamped in the midst of sugar plantations, and a considerable portion of his new ramparts was formed of hogsheads of sugar, set on end.

When day dawned, and the Americans saw thirty guns frowning down upon them from high bastions that had risen as if by magic in the darkness, the sight was rather appalling ; but as soon as fire was opened upon these apparently formidable works, it was seen that the balls passed right through the hogsheads of sugar, and the whole fabric began to crumble away. There was also a vulnerable element in Jackson's works ; for he had used cotton bales as his enemy used sugar, and though the cotton resisted the passage of a ball, it was easily set on fire, and the bales knocked out of position.

Commodore Patterson had erected a battery on the opposite bank of the Mississippi, to rake the ground held by the British, who at the same time had erected one on the levee to oppose it. For an hour these guns were all blazing at once ; and when the firing ceased and the smoke rolled away, it was found that the British works had been completely ruined, and seventy of their men killed or wounded ; the American works were not seriously damaged, but they had lost thirty-four men.

Jackson made haste to throw away his cotton bales, supply their place with earth, and construct a second line of works a mile and a half in the rear, and for a week nervously awaited the next move of the enemy. In that week he was joined by nearly three thousand Kentucky and Louisiana militia ; but as they were in rags and had scarcely a firelock among them, they could hardly be considered a reënforcement. The British were reënforced by two regiments under General John Lambert.

Pakenham's final plan was to send a heavy force across the river to capture Patterson's batteries and turn them upon Jackson's lines, and at the same time push forward the remainder of his force to assault those lines in front, the advance guard to fill the ditch with fascines and plant scaling-ladders against the ramparts. Preparatory to this, it was necessary to dig a canal across the isthmus, to drag boats through from Lake Borgne to the Mississippi, and this occupied his troops nearly six days.

On Saturday, January 7th, Jackson stood upon the tallest building within his lines, and through a large spy-glass which a planter had mounted for him, saw the red-coats making fascines by binding up sheaves of sugar-cane, and constructing ladders. At the same time, Pakenham was surveying the American works from the top of a pine-tree.

The British general intended to make an attack on both sides of the river simultaneously, before daylight on the 8th. But there was great difficulty in navigating the canal, the sides of which had caved in ; only enough boats were brought through to carry over five hundred troops, instead of fourteen hundred, and these were delayed several hours. A detachment under Colonel Thornton embarked in them, but were swept down by the current and reached the western shore far below the intended landing-place.

Meanwhile the sun had risen, the fog was rolling away, Pakenham was impatient, and before Thornton could get near his enemy he saw the signal rocket which announced the attack. The Americans understood the signal quite as well as he did, and were ready to meet the shock. One thirty-two pounder was loaded to the muzzle with musket-balls. A deserter had told the British commander that the weak spot in Jackson's line was the extreme left ; true enough when he said it, but now that spot was strengthened by two thousand Tennessee and Kentucky riflemen. The heaviest attack was accordingly made at this point, a column of three thousand men, under General Gibbs, moving against it. They were to be preceded by an Irish regiment bearing the fascines and ladders. At the same time, a column of one thousand moved along the river road, under the cross-fire from Patterson's battery, to attack Jackson's right. These were to be preceded by a West India black regiment with the necessary fascines and ladders. Midway between stood nearly a thousand Highlanders, under General Keane, ready to support either column, as circumstances might require. The British had also a battery of six eighteen-pounders ; and, drawn up behind all, a considerable reserve.

The battle was what Bunker Hill would have been if the Americans had had stronger works and plenty of ammunition. The beautiful British columns moved forward only to be mowed down. When the thirty-two pounder discharged its musket-balls, the head of one column melted away before it, two hundred men being disabled. Both the Irish and the Negro regiment failed in their duty, so that when the main columns arrived at the ditch they had no means of crossing, and the terrible blunder had to be remedied under a continuous and withering fire. The ranks were badly broken. Pakenham, trying to re-form them, was killed, falling into the arms of Captain McDougall, the same officer who had caught General Ross when he fell at North Point. General Gibbs was wounded mortally ; General Keane seriously. Colonel Dale fell at the head of the Highland regiment, which was almost entirely destroyed. It went into the fight with over nine hundred men, and came out with one hundred and forty. A major and a lieutenant, with twenty men, crossed the ditch before the American left, and the two officers mounted the breastwork. The major was instantly riddled with bullets ; the lieutenant demanded the swords of two officers who confronted him, and was told to look behind him. He turned, and saw, as he expressed it, that the men he supposed to be following " had vanished as if the earth had opened and swallowed them up."

On the American right, the British carried a small outwork ; but the guns of the main line were turned upon it and cleared it.   Of this column, only three men — a colonel, a major, and a captain — reached the breastwork, and as they mounted they were all shot and tumbled into the ditch together.

The action lasted but twenty-five minutes.   Seven hundred of the British were killed, fourteen hundred wounded, and five hundred prisoners.   The Americans lost four killed and thirteen wounded ; in the entire campaign, three hundred and thirty-three.

The force under Thornton, on the western bank of the river, carried the American works, where but brief resistance was made, and were pursuing the retreating militia, when news of the disaster on the other bank was brought to Thornton, together with an order to return.   He had lost a hundred men, killed or wounded, and inflicted a loss of but six.

The 9th was spent, under an armistice, in burying the dead and caring for the wounded. General Lambert then determined to withdraw to the shipping and abandon the enterprise, but was ten days about it, during which time his troops were annoyed by incessant cannonading by day and " hunting parties" by night.   The British fleet had entered the Mississippi at its mouth, and from the 10th to the 17th bombarded Fort St. Philip, seventy-five miles below New Orleans, but effected nothing, and on the 18th withdrew.

CHAPTER XXI.

PEACE.

The Treaty of Ghent—Treatment of Prisoners—Losses and Gains
by the War—Conclusion.

HAD there been an Atlantic cable, or even a
transatlantic steamer, with land telegraphs, in those
days, the slaughter before New Orleans might have
been prevented ; for a treaty of peace had been
signed at Ghent on the 24th of December, 1814.
It made the usual stipulations for the exchange of
prisoners and the return of property, guaranteed
peace to the Indians, and provided for a settlement
by commissioners of questions as to boundary and
the islands in Passamaquoddy Bay, — and it provided for little else. The negotiations had been
going on for five months, and more than once were
in danger of being broken off on account of the
insolent and supercilious bearing of the English
Commissioners. So says Adams in his diary.

At the outset, the British Commissioners had insisted that the Indians should have a territory set off
to them, as neutral ground between the British
and the American possessions, and that the United
States should have no armament on the great lakes

and no fortifications on their shores, while Canada
was not to be restricted. On the other hand, the
American Commissioners had insisted on formal ab-
rogation of the right of search and impressment.
But all these points were ultimately given up. As
early as June the American Commissioners had
been instructed by the President that they might
omit any stipulation on the subject of impressment,
if it was found indispensably necessary to do so in
order to terminate the war ; and acting under this
instruction they yielded to the argument that, as
Europe was now at peace, there was no longer any
occasion for exercising the right, and therefore no
practical necessity for mentioning it.

The treaty was severely criticised and mercilessly
ridiculed as a meaningless document. It might
have been answered that the Federalists at least had
no right to complain, since they had clamored only
for peace, and the treaty brought peace. Better
than this, it might have been answered that when a
point has been practically settled by war, it is of
little consequence whether it is conceded on paper ;
since every nation is likely to heed a lesson taught
by force of arms, and equally likely, when interest
dictates, to abrogate a treaty ; and, whatever might
be said of the campaigns on land, it could not be
denied that American mariners had abundantly vin-

dicated their right to an unmolested navigation of the high seas — a right which British cruisers have never since interfered with.

There had been no exchange of prisoners during the war, though many had been paroled, and there were bitter complaints of the treatment received by Americans in British prisons. This was especially true of those confined at Dartmoor, the most unhealthful spot in the dreary highlands of Devonshire. These men were not only not released, but were not even informed that peace had been concluded, till three months after the treaty was signed. There seemed to be a special spite against them because they were mostly American sailors, who had audaciously and successfully disputed England's sovereignty of the seas.

If it be a matter of pride, as an English poetess appears to think, for a nation to strew its dead over the face of the globe,* then Great Britain certainly won fresh laurels in this war ; for her soldiers who fell in it found graves six thousand miles apart: in the depths of Lake Erie, about the great falls of Niagara, and along the Thames and St. Lawrence ; in the Atlantic, both near the American coast and almost within sight of their own shores ; in Long

---

* Wave may not foam, nor wild wind sweep,
  Where rest not England's dead.—*Mrs. Hemans.*

Island Sound, in the Chesapeake, and beyond the western edge of civilization ; before the defences of Baltimore and New Orleans, and in the waters of the South Pacific.   And her expeditions had been especially fatal to their commanders : Gen. Brock had fallen at Queenstown, Gen. Tecumseh at the Thames, Ross and Sir Peter Parker before Baltimore, Pakenham and Gibbs at New Orleans, with many of lower rank but hardly less responsibility ; while seven commanders of her men-of-war — Lambert, Downie, Dickenson, Manners, Peake, Barrette, and Blythe — had all died on their bloody decks.   But by her sacrifice of life and property she had gained absolutely nothing.   She had not acquired an inch of territory, or established any principle of international law, or purchased for herself any new privilege, or secured any old one.   The war had cost the United States a hundred million dollars in money, and thirty thousand lives ; and a large portion of both the money and the lives had been squandered, when with ordinary skill and care they might have been saved.   But she had something to show for it.   If she had not fully relieved her frontier of the atrocities of the Indians, she had at least cut off their supplies from British sources, and possessed herself of all the western posts ; she had put an end to the systematic violation of her rights on the ocean, and in so doing had demonstrated the superiority of American seamanship ; she had completely established her national independence.

It is to be hoped that no American youth who reads this little history will cherish any feeling of resentment or hatred toward the people whose fathers were so grievously unjust to ours.   The day for that — if ever there was a day for it — has gone completely by.   England has evidently passed the zenith of her power and glory ; America is still rising toward hers, and how great she shall ultimately become, will be measured mainly by the breadth and generosity of the American mind.   In the past sixty years we have lived down the most celebrated sneer in history.   Five years after this war, the Rev. Sydney Smith wrote in the *Edinburgh Review :* "In the four quarters of the globe, who reads an American book ? or goes to an American play ? or looks at an American picture or statue?   What does the world yet owe to American physicians or surgeons?   What new substances have their chemists discovered, or what old ones have they analyzed ?   What new constellations have been discovered by the telescopes of Americans?   What have they done in mathematics?   Who drinks out of American glasses, or eats from American plates, or wears American coats or gowns, or sleeps in

American blankets? Finally, under which of the old tyrannical governments of Europe is every sixth man a slave, whom his fellow citizens may buy and sell and torture?'' If Mr. Smith were now living, he might be answered — if it were worth while to answer him at all — that the most widely circulated of all novels was written by an American woman; that the poet most read in England was an American; that our two standard dictionaries of the English language are both American; that several American magazines count their subscribers in Great Britain by tens of thousands; that the world owes its use of anæsthetics to an American physician; that American sculptors, painters, and actors hold their own with those of other nations; that America has the largest telescopes, and the most successful astronomers; that American reapers cut the world's harvests, and American sewing machines make its garments; that the telegraph and the telephone are American inventions; that the first steamboat was built in America, and it was an American steamship that first crossed the Atlantic, while our country contains more miles of railway than all Europe; that those who eat from American plates, eat the largest and best dinners in the world; and as for American glasses, altogether too many people drink out of them. Unless we mercifully left his final

question unanswered, we should be obliged to say,
that the United States had gotten rid of slavery,
while to-day five million British subjects, all within
two days' journey of the throne, tell us they find
themselves virtually slaves.

Yet with all our material and intellectual progress,
we have hardly a right to be proud. For we have
enjoyed peculiar advantages. The *Mayflower* did
not land her pilgrims on a narrow island, but on
the edge of a great continent. Of that continent
we have the most productive zone, stretching from
ocean to ocean, and a thousand miles in breadth ;
while within that zone our Government has given
us, for the support of educational institutions, as
much land as the entire area of Great Britain and
Ireland. At the same time, we have not been loaded
down with a standing army, an established church,
a vast landed aristocracy, and all the rubbish of
royalty. In America labor receives its highest
wages, and pauperism finds its least excuse. It will
be no special credit to us if we become in the next
half century the most powerful and prosperous and
generous of nations ; but it will be a great shame to
us if we do not.

As we read the history of our country's early
struggles, it may help us to avoid any unworthy
feeling of resentment if we bear in mind the fact

that there is a wide and peculiar discrepancy of character between the English people and the English Government. That people, perhaps at present the most enlightened on earth, are justly noted for their innate love of fair play, for their continual struggles toward liberty, and their development of the great principles of jurisprudence ; but that Government, in its dealings with other powers, has been for centuries arbitrary, selfish, barbarous, and inconsistent to the last degree. Priding itself upon legitimacy, it has befriended a bloody usurpation in France, because it hated the alternative of French republicanism. It has opened the ports of China with its cannon, for the purpose of selling there a narcotic drug of which it holds the monopoly. It boasted its abolition of the slave trade ; yet when our country was at war over the slavery question, its sympathies were all with the slaveholders. Seventy years ago, as we have seen, its cruisers cared nothing for the neutrality of any harbor in which a hostile ship of fewer guns was riding at anchor ; but twenty years ago it could not offer its neutral hospitalities too lavishly to privateers that had not a port of their own to hail from or sail to, and were burning all their prizes at sea without adjudication. It witnessed the dismemberment of Denmark with scarcely a protest, but has sacrificed thousands of English lives to maintain the Turk in Europe. It has stood for years at the head of a great conspiracy to keep Russia shut up in the centre of a continent long after her industrial growth and commercial importance have entitled her to a broad and unobstructed outlet to the highway of nations. It has eaten India into famine, and is now laying its kleptic fingers on the great island of Borneo, and apparently making ready to consume the continent of Africa.

We must blush for these things while we execrate them; for we ourselves are Englishmen. That famous little island, with its green lanes and waving woodlands, its busy towns and historical hamlets, was the home of our ancestors, and must ever have for us the highest romantic interest of any spot on earth; and we cannot too warmly sympathize with those who are still bearing burdens of feudal days, when the bravery of feudal leadership has long since passed away. Let us never forget how near of kin we are to the English people; but God forbid that we should inherit the vices of the English Government, or copy its crimes!

If the story of a war like that we have been reading of teaches anything, it teaches the broad wisdom of dealing justly, and the ultimate folly of all chicanery, violence, and wrong.